intros, endings & turnarounds
FOR KEYBOARD

by John Valerio

ISBN 978-0-634-02301-9

HAL•LEONARD®
CORPORATION

Preface

This book offers a number of ideas for creating introductions, endings, and turnarounds. Fake books and lead sheets usually do not include these essential elements of jazz/pop performance. The materials found in this book are based on common practice. The reader will gain an understanding of the processes involved in creating intros, endings, and turnarounds, and will also be given specific examples.

It is assumed that the reader has a basic knowledge and understanding of jazz/pop theory, particularly chords and their relationships. The examples in this book will include jazz/pop chord symbols and Roman numeral notation. The jazz/pop symbols are those commonly found in fake books and lead sheets. The Roman numeral notation is the kind commonly used in jazz theory, as opposed to that commonly used in classical music theory. All chord symbols use upper case numerals, and each chord symbol relates to the prevailing key rather than to temporary modulations. For example, in the key of C major a D7 chord is notated as II7 and not as V7 of V. Also, each Roman numeral indication is qualified: IIm7 indicates a minor 7th chord, II7 indicates a dominant 7th chord, etc. All scale degrees are absolute and relate directly to the tonic. Thus, in the key of C minor, VI7 indicates A7, and ♭VI7 indicates A♭7; IIIm7 indicates Em7, and ♭IIIm7 indicates E♭m7, etc.

Since there is no standard way of indicating inversions with Roman numerals in jazz/pop notation, the following method will be employed: A Roman numeral after a slash indicates the scale degree that is the lowest note of the chord. Thus, in C major, I/III = C/E and IV7/VI = F7/A. The numeral after the slash does not indicate a polychord. This system is a bit bulky, but it should be clear.

In major keys, I chords can be major triads, major 7th, or major 6th chords. In minor keys, I chords can be minor triads, minor-major 7th chords, or minor 6th chords. Any alternative can be used for each key, and they are essentially interchangeable for the examples in this book.

Each example comes with chord symbols and Roman numeral analysis for easy transposition. The chord symbols are kept simple for the most part, and extensions and alterations that appear in the examples are not always indicated in chord symbols. The Roman numeral symbols are only those of the basic chord.

The reader should try each intro and ending example first as written, and then transposed to several keys. After one is comfortable with each examples, new intros and endings based on the chord progression for each example should be invented. These can be written out or improvised. The turnaround progressions should be tried in all keys.

The book is divided into three parts: 1) intros, 2) endings, and 3) turnarounds. Many of the intros used are based on standard turnarounds. Although the intros are presented first, the reader may wish to examine the turnarounds beforehand, or in conjunction with the intros.

The material offered here is only a sampling and serves more as a source for ideas than a definitive reference.

Contents

PART 1
INTRODUCTIONS

The purpose of an introduction is to set the tempo, tonality, and mood of a tune. Most intros in a basic swing or "straight-ahead" style are either four or eight measures long. Occasionally a two-measure intro is used, especially for slower tempos. A good intro should not only set up the ensuing tonality but also lead convincingly to the first chord of the tune. Most tunes from the jazz/pop standard era begin on a I chord, but many begin on a II, IV, or VI chord; any chord is possible. The most obvious and common way to lead to the opening chord is to precede it by its V7 (dominant) chord or, in other words, by a dominant seventh chord with a root that is a perfect 5th above the root of the target chord. Various substitutions for the preceding V7 can be used as well.

The simplest and perhaps most often used intros are based on simple standard turnarounds. Turnarounds are harmonic formulas used most often at the end of a tune or section of a tune to lead back to the beginning of the tune or new section. They are also used to connect chords in a static harmonic progression. Turnarounds can be built into the tune or improvised during performance. The following examples present sample intros for medium- to fast- or slow- to medium-tempo traditional/swing and jazz/pop standard tunes.

Swing • Major Keys
Intros for Tunes Starting on I Chords

The strongest harmonic relationship in traditional tonal music is V-I, the movement from dominant to tonic. Most classical tonal compositions are based around a I-V-I framework. The departure from tonic to dominant and resolution back to the tonic is the structural foundation of all tonal music. This relationship can occur on the local level (beat to beat or measure to measure), as well as the long-term level. A I-V progression serves as a logical introduction for a tune starting on a I chord. In most jazz settings the V chord is usually preceded by a II chord which serves as a dominant preparation. The most basic introduction for tunes starting on I chords is: I-II-V. Two examples in C major and F major follow.

Basic Turnaround Intros

| Imaj7 | | | IIm7 | V7 | to I

A common variation on the I-II-V progression is I-VI-II-V. Here the VI chord replaces the I chord in the second measure. The VIm7 chord often acts as a tonic substitute. This common intro chord progression is also a typical turnaround and a regular chord progression found in many tunes:

| Imaj7 | VIm7 | IIm7 | V7 | to I

The preceding progression will serve as a basic model for the next several examples. The qualities of the VI and II chords can be changed to dominant seventh chords as follows:

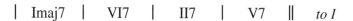

Tritone substitutions can be used for any of the dominant 7th chords. A dominant 7th chord with a root a tritone away can usually substitute for any other dominant 7th chord. Thus D♭7 can substitute for G7 and vice versa, A7 and E♭7 can substitute for each other, etc. The following examples present several variations on the basic I-VI-II-V model:

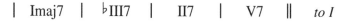

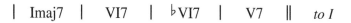

| Imaj7 | ♭III7 | ♭VI7 | ♭II7 ‖ *to I*

In some introductions/turnarounds, major 7th chords are used instead of dominant 7th chords for the root progression used above.

| Imaj7 | ♭IIImaj7 | ♭VImaj7 | ♭IImaj7 ‖ *to I*

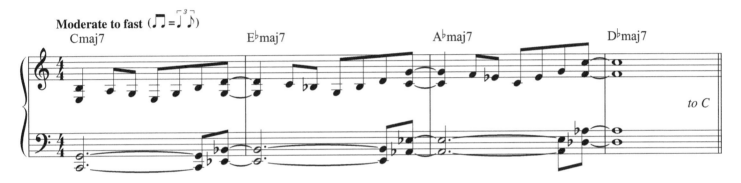

A combination of dominant and major 7th chords can also be used:

| Imaj7 | ♭III7 | ♭VImaj7 | V7 ‖ *to I*

In many introduction/turnaround situations, a III chord can freely substitute for a I chord in the basic I-VI-II-V model.

| IIIm7 | VI7 | IIm7 | V7 ‖ *to I*

As in standard turnarounds, diminished chords can substitute for the VI chord. Diminished 7th chords built on ♯I and ♭III are the most common:

| Imaj7 | ♯Idim | IIm7 | V7 || *to I*

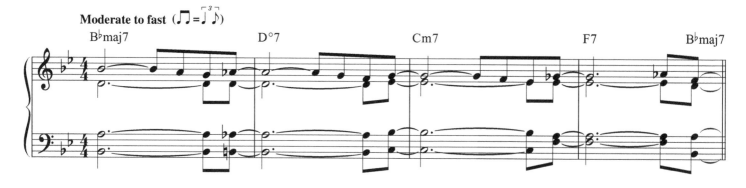

Note that the ♭IIIdim7 chord is written here enharmonically as F♯°7:

| Imaj7 | ♭IIIdim7 | IIm7 | V7 || *to I*

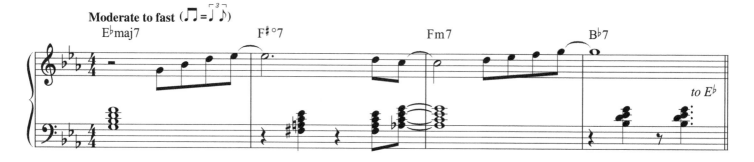

Any of the above progressions can be repeated or combined by changing the harmonic rhythm to half notes. The following examples offer several possibilities:

| Imaj7–VI7 | IIm7–V7 | IIIm7–VI7 | IIm7–♭II7 || *to I*

| Imaj7–VI7 | IIm7–V7 | IIIm7–♭III7 | IIm7–♭II | ‖   *to I*

| IIIm7–VI7 | IIm7–V7 | IIIm7–♭III7 | IIm7–♭II7 | ‖   *to I*

Note that the ♯IIdim7 chord acts as a passing chord between IIm7 and IIIm7, as well as a substitute for V of III (E7):

| I6–♯Idim7 | IIm7–♯IIdim7 | IIIm7–VI7 | IIm7–V7 | ‖   *to I*

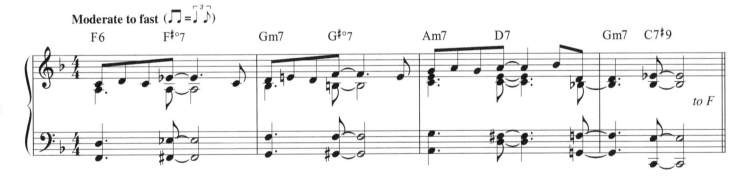

| I–VIm7 | IIm7–V7 | IIIm7–♭III7 | IIm7–V7 | ‖   *to I*

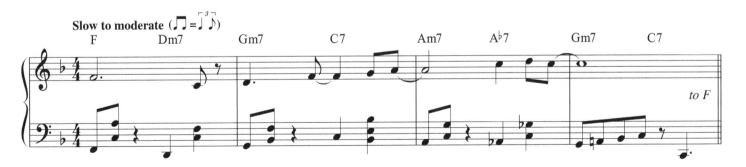

Other Intro Models

Formulas other than the I-VI-II-V model are often used for tunes that begin on I chords. Some samples follow:

I-IV Progressions

Here are two examples that begin with a I-IV movement:

| Imaj7 | IV7 | IIIm7–VI7 | IIm7–V7 ‖   *to I*

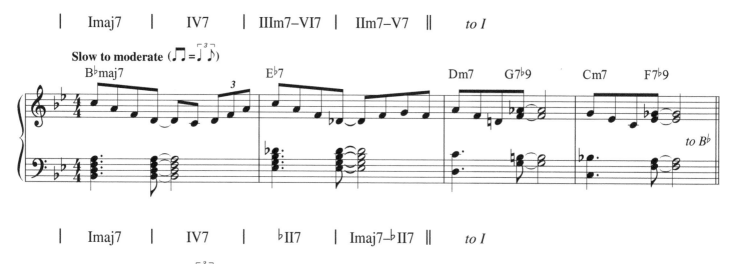

| Imaj7 | IV7 | ♭II7 | Imaj7–♭II7 ‖   *to I*

Diatonic Progressions

Here are three examples that feature mostly diatonic stepwise movement:

| Imaj7–IIm7 | IIIm7–♭III7 | IIm7 | V7 ‖   *to I*

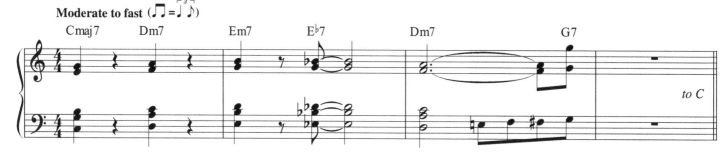

10

| Imaj7–IIm7 | IIIm7–♭III7 | IIm7–IIIm7 | IVmaj7–V7 ‖   to I

| Imaj7–IIm7 | IIIm7–VI7 | IIm7–IIIm7–IVmaj7–♯IVdim7 | V7 ‖   to I

Beginning on II Chords

Intros for tunes that start on I chords do not have to begin with I chords. The following two intros begin with II-V-I progressions:

| IIm7 | V7 | I | V7 ‖   to I

| IIm7 | V7 | Imaj7–♭VII7 | ♭VI7–V7 ‖   to I

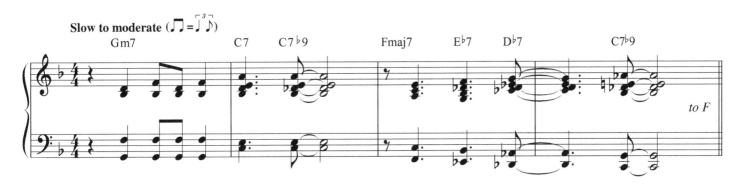

Beginning on ♭VII Chords

Chords can progress to I by starting on a ♭VII7 chord. This first example uses a repeating chromatic progression:

| ♭VII7–VI7 | ♭VI7–V7 | ♭VII7–VI7 | ♭VI7–V7 ‖   *to I*

The next example is based on the circle of descending fifths:

| ♭VII7 | ♭III7 | ♭VI7 | ♭II7 ‖   *to I*

Starting on a m7♭5 Chord

Intros can begin on a m7♭5 chord. Usually these are IIm7♭5, IIIm7♭5, or ♭Vm7♭5. IIm7♭5 is usually a II chord in minor keys but is often used in major keys. IIm7♭5 can substitute for IIm7 in many of the preceding progressions. Melodic considerations must be taken into account when doing so.

| IIm7♭5 | V7 | Imaj7–VI7 | IIm7♭5–V7   ‖   *to I*

The next example is a variation on the IIIm7-VI7-IIm7-V7 variation of the I-VI-II-V model:

| IIIm7♭5 | VI7 | IIm7♭5 | V7 ‖ to I |

The next progression is also used for a common ending, starting on ♭Vm7♭5:

| ♭Vm7♭5–IVm7 | IIIm7–♭III7 | IIm7 | V7 ‖ to I |

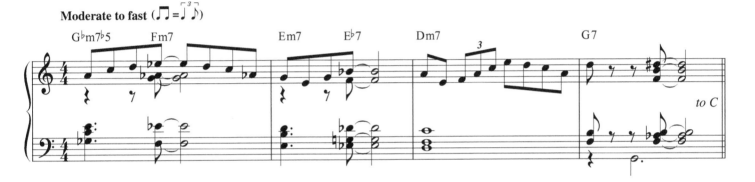

Circle of Fifths Progressions

Typical of many tunes, intros may progress around the descending circle of 5ths in various ways. Two examples follow:

| Imaj7–IVmaj7 | ♭VIImaj7–♭IIImaj7 | ♭VImaj7 | ♭II7 ‖ to I |

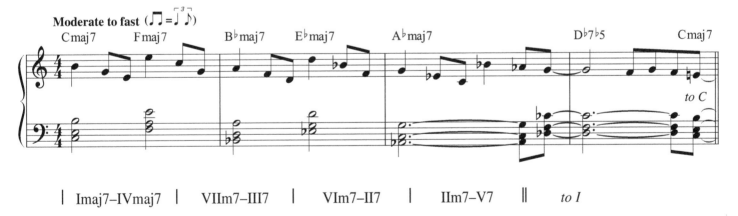

| Imaj7–IVmaj7 | VIIm7–III7 | VIm7–II7 | IIm7–V7 ‖ to I |

Stepwise Progressions

Intros can make use of whole- or half-step progressions. Two examples follow:

| Imaj7–♭VIImaj7 | ♭VImaj7–V7–Imaj7–♭VIImaj7 | ♭VImaj7–V7 ‖   *to I*

| Imaj7–VII7 | ♭VI7–VI7 | IIm7–IIm7–IV6–♯IVm7♭5 | V7   ‖   *to I*

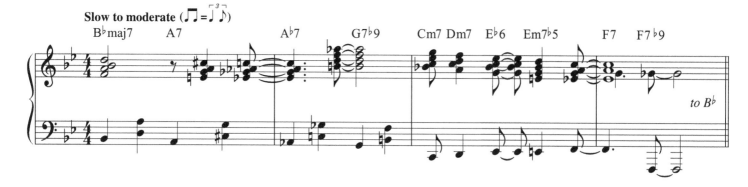

Mixed and Miscellaneous Progressions

Below are several intros that combine some of the progression types used above and add a few twists:

| Imaj7–♭IIImaj7 | ♭VImaj7–♭IImaj7 | I6–♭VII6 | ♭VI6–V7   ‖   *to I*

| I6–♭V7 | IV7–♭III7 | IIIm7–VI7 | IIm7–V7 ‖   *to I*

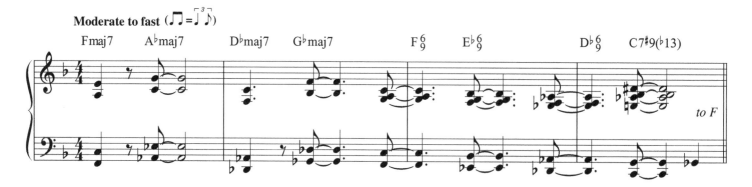

| Imaj7–♭VIm7 | IIm7–V7 | IIIm7♭5–VI7 | IIm7–V7 ‖ *to I*

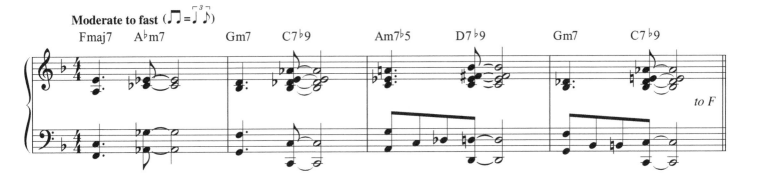

Parallel Dominant Seventh Chords

Intros can start on a I7 chord and proceed to V7 through a series dominant 7th chords. Two examples follow:

| I7 | ♭VII7 | ♭VI7 | V7–IV7–♯IV7–V7 ‖ *to I*

| I7–VII7 | ♭VII7–VI7 | ♭VI | V7 ‖ *to I*

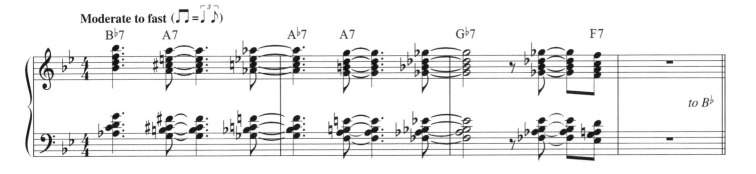

Swing • Major Keys

Intros for Tunes Starting on II Chords

Many tunes start on a II chord of some kind, usually a IIm7, II7, or IIm7♭5. Most of the intros for tunes starting on I chords can also be used for tunes starting on II chords. Even though the V7 or ♭II7 chords that end these intros naturally progress to a I chord, they work just as well progressing to a II chord which usually moves eventually through a V chord to a I chord. The effect here is one of delayed resolution. This section focuses on intros that progress to and center on the II chord.

Intros for tunes that start on II chords can begin on a I chord and lead directly to a II chord. The II chord is usually led to through a VI7 chord that acts as a dominant or V chord of the II chord. The term for this is secondary dominant, or V of II chord. Thus in the key of C major, the II chord (Dm7) is typically preceded by its V7 chord (A7), which is also VI7 in C major.

I to II Progressions

Many intros lead from I to II chords through standard turnaround progressions. In these situations, the II chord is approached by a secondary dominant 7th chord or by a substitute chord.

The following three examples present simple ways of going from I to II in an introduction. Most of these intros will work for a tune starting on a IIm7 chord, a II7 chord, or even a IIm7♭5 in major.

| Imaj7 | IVmaj7 | IIIm7 | VI7 ‖ *to II*

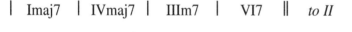

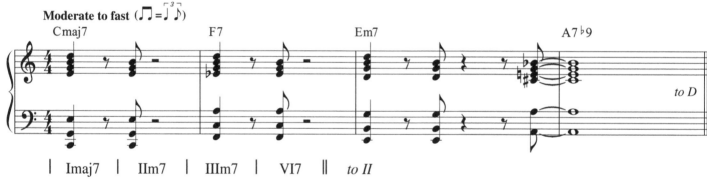

| Imaj7 | IIm7 | IIIm7 | VI7 ‖ *to II*

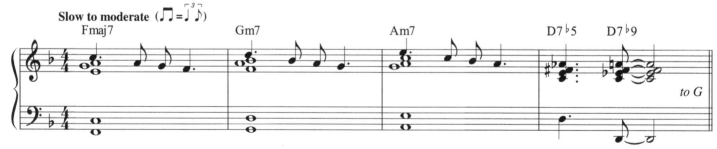

| Imaj7 | VII7 | ♭VII7 | VI7 ‖ *to II*

The use of a IVm7-♭VII7 movement within an intro progression can create interest and a sense of mystery. Two examples follow:

| Imaj7 | IIm7–IIIm7 | IVm7–♭VII7 | IIm7–♭III7 ‖ *to II*

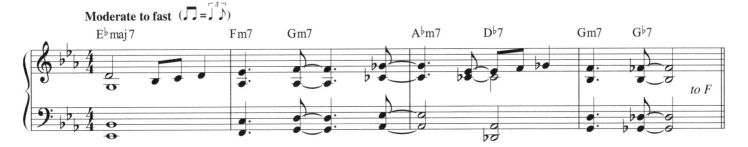

| Imaj7–IIm7 | #IIdim7–IIIm7 | IVm7 –♭VII7 | IIIm7–VI ‖ *to II*

Descending Bass Lines

Using chords derived from a stepwise descending bass line can create interesting progressions.

The following progression uses a descending bass line that begins diatonically and ends with a chromatic "push" to the II chord.

| Imaj7–III7/VII | VIm7–VIm7/V | ♭Vm7♭5–III7 | IIm7–♭II7 ‖ *to II*

Parallel Chord Movement

Intros can contain several chords that move in parallel for the most part.

The following three examples feature parallel I and ♭VI chords:

| Imaj7 | ♭VImaj7 | Imaj7–♭VIImaj7 | V7 ‖ *to II*

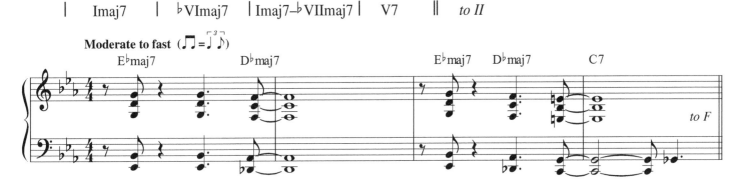

| I7–VII7 | ♭VII7–VII7 | I7–♭VII7 | VI7 ‖ *to II*

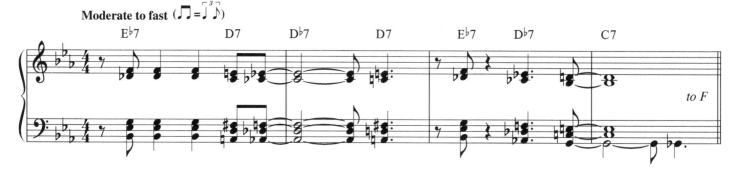

| I7 | ♭VII7 | IIIm7 | V7 ‖ *to II*

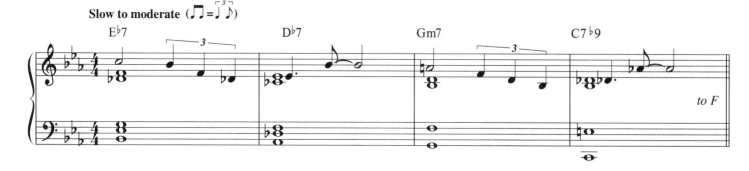

Intros that Begin on II Chords

Intros for tunes that start on II chords often begin on II chords.

The basic I-VI-II-V model can be shifted around to produce a basic model for intros or turnarounds leading to a II chord. Several variations follow:

| IIm7 | V7 | Imaj7 | VI7 ‖ *to II*

The following is an intro for a medium ballad:

| IIm7 | V7 | IIIm7 | V7 ‖ *to II*

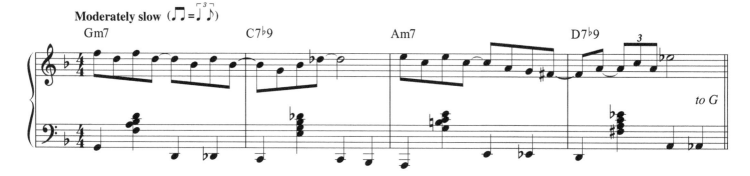

The following three progressions combine II-V-I progressions with common turnarounds:

| IIm7 | V7 | Imaj7–IV7 | IIm7–VI7 ‖ *to II*

| IIm7 | V7 | I7–VII7 | ♭VII–VI7 ‖ *to II*

The next example begins on a II dominant 7th and works well with tunes that begin on a II7 chord:

| II7 | V7 | I6–IV7 | IIIm7–♭III7 ‖ *to II*

The following three examples present variations on a common progression beginning with IIm7-♯Idim7-IIm7–V7. The use of ♯Idim7 between the two IIm7 acts like a dominant of II and tends to focus the progression on IIm7:

| IIm7–♯Idim7 | IIm7–V7 | I6–IV7 | IIIm7–VI7 ‖ *to IIm7*

| IIm7–#Idim7 | IIm7–V7 | I6–VII7 | ♭VII7–VI7 ‖ *to IIm7*

The next variation leads directly from I to II through a walking bass line:

| IIm7–#Idim7 | IIm7–V7 | I6 | ‖ *to IIm7*

II Approached through ♭III

IIm7 chords can be approached directly through a ♭IIIm7 or a ♭IIIm7–♭VI7 movement. Three examples follow:

| IIm7 | V7 | IIIm7 | ♭IIIm7–♭VI7 ‖ *to II*

| IIm7–V7 | IIm7–V7 | IVm7–♭VII7 | IIIm7–♭IIIm7 ‖ *to II*

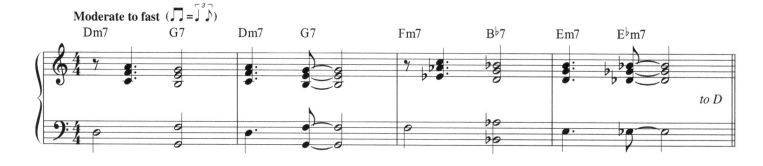

| IIm7–V7 | IVm7–♭VII7 | IIIm7–VI7 | ♭IIIm7–VI7 ‖ *to II*

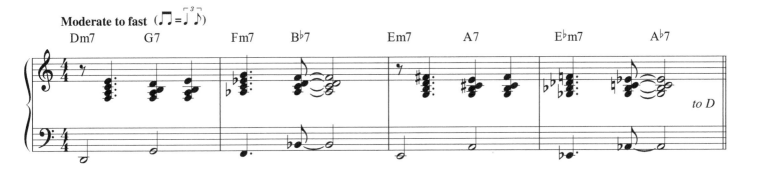

| IIm7 | IVm7 | IIIm7 | ♭III7 ‖ *to II*

Starting on ♭V

A II chord can be approached through a progression beginning with a ♭Vm7♭5 chord. The similarity between a ♭Vm7♭5 chord and a II7 (dominant 7th) chord make these intros nicely suited for tunes that start on a II7 chord. Two examples follow:

| ♭Vm7♭5 | IVm7 | IIIm7 | VI7 ‖ *to II*

| ♭Vm7♭5 | VII7 | IIIm7♭5 | VI7 ‖ *to II*

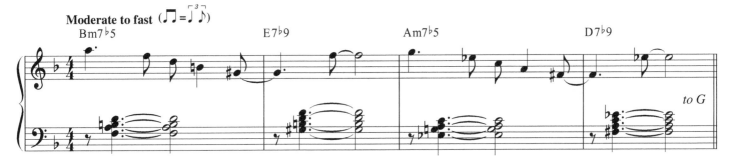

Swing • Major Keys
Intros for Tunes Starting on VI Chords

Some tunes start on VI chords, most often VIm7. Since a minor VI chord is the relative minor of any major I chord, intros and turnarounds can progress easily from I to VI. Intros for tunes starting on a VI chord are generally approached two different ways: The intro can focus on the VI chord as if the initial key were minor, or it can progress from the tonic major key to VI in various ways. (See Section 5 for introductions in minor keys for the first approach.) This section will focus on intros that progress from the tonic major key to the VIm7 chord.

A simple way to establish a major tonality and progress to a VIm7 chord is to start on I and move directly to VI. The example that follows presents a typical "tonicization" of VI through a minor key II-V movement. The Em7♭5-A7 progression, which is VIIm7♭5-III7 in F major, acts like IIm7♭5-V7 in D minor:

| Imaj7 | VIm7 | VIIm7♭5 | III7 || *to VI*

The following two examples progress from I to IV before moving to VI in a similar way as the example above. This creates a circle of descending fifths.

| Imaj7 | IVmaj7 | VIIm7♭5 | III7 || *to VI*

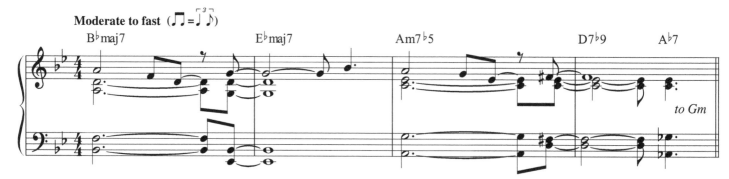

The next intro uses a ♭VII7 chord as a substitute for III7 to lead to VI.

| Imaj7 | VImaj7 | VIIm7♭5 | ♭VII7 || *to VI*

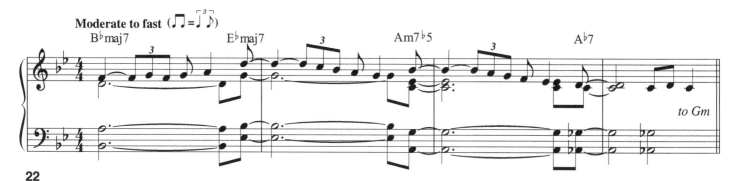

Starting on VI

An intro that leads to VI can also start on a VI chord and progress to I before leading back to VI. Two examples follow.

This intro features a walking bass line:

| VIm7 | IIm7 | V7 | Imaj7–III7 ‖ to VI

In this example, the VIm7-II7 progression acts like a II-V of V but eventually leads back to VI:

| VIm7–II7 | VIm7–II7 | IIm7–V7 | Imaj7–VIIm7♭5–♭VII7 ‖ to VI

Moving to III7

A simple movement to III7 (V7 of VI) at the end of any intro that begins its last measure on a I chord can be used for tunes that begin on a VI chord.

| ♭Vm7♭5–IVm7 | IIIm7–♭IIIdim7 | IIm7–V7 | I6–III7 ‖ to VI

The next example moves toward a IIImaj7 chord that becomes a III7 chord—which acts as a dominant chord of VI.

| IIm7–V7 | IIIm7♭5–VI7 |♭Vm7♭5–VII7 | IIImaj7–III7 ‖ to VI

Focusing on III7

The next example presents a progression that elaborates on a III7 chord that acts as a V of VI:

| | III7 | | VIIm7/#IV | | IIIm7♭5 | | III7/#V | ‖ | *to VI* |

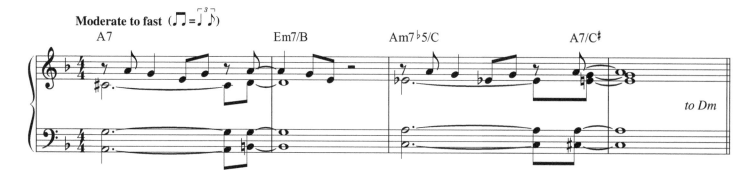

Leading to a Dominant VI Chord

Some tunes start on a VI7 (dominant 7th) chord. Two examples follow.

In this first intro, the descending chromatic movement of dominant 7th chords from I to VI (at the beginning and the end) help to establish the VI7 at the start of a tune.

| | I6–VII7 | | ♭VII7–VI7 | | II7–V7 | | I6–VII7–♭VII7 | ‖ | *to VI7* |

In the next intro, the IIm7 chord in the IIm7-V7 of VI (VIIm7-III7) progression helps establish the VI7 chord more effectively than a IIm7♭5 would.

| | Imaj7 | | IIm7–V7 | | Imaj7 | | VIIm7–III7 | ‖ | *to VI7* |

Swing • Major Keys
Intros for Tunes Starting on IV Chords

Some tunes start on IV chords. These are usually major but can also be minor. As before, any intro that directs the progression toward the first chord can be used. The IV chord is most often set up through the dominant chord built on the tonic root (I7), which acts as a V of IV, or its substitute (♭V7), which acts as a ♭II of IV.

I-VI-Vm7-I7 Progressions

The I-VI-Vm7-I7 progression leading to IV can serve as a model that can be varied in many ways. Three examples follow.

The first example inserts a passing chord between VIm7 and Vm7:

| Imaj7 | VIm7–♭VI7 | Vm7–I7 || *to IV*

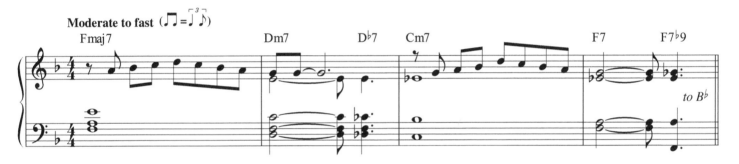

The next example uses a diminished chord on VI:

| Imaj7 | VIdim7 | Vm7 | ♭V7 || *to IV*

This variation uses a ♭VI7 chord:

| Imaj7 | ♭VI7 | Vm7 | I7 || *to IV*

Circle of Fifths Progressions

Going around the circle of descending fifths can produce more elaborate progressions. An example follows. Note that the Dm7 chord in the third measure delays the movement to G7. This is a common harmonic motion:

| Imaj7–IV7 | IIIm7–VI7 | VIm7–II7 | Vm7–♭V7 ‖ *to IV*

Descending Stepwise Progressions

The movement from I to IV can go through a stepwise descending progression. The following two examples offer different ways of doing this.

This first intro presents a chromatic descending progression:

| Imaj7 |VIIm7♭5–♭VII| VIm7–♭VI7 | Vm7–♭V7 ‖ *to IV*

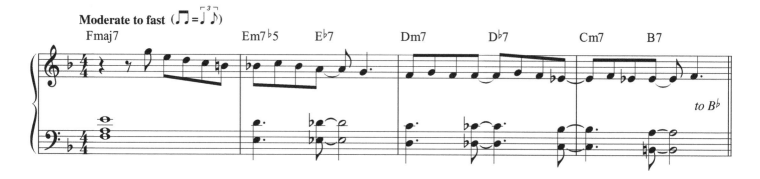

The next progression proceeds in descending whole steps:

| Imaj7 | ♭VII7 | ♭VImaj7 | ♭V7 ‖ *to IV*

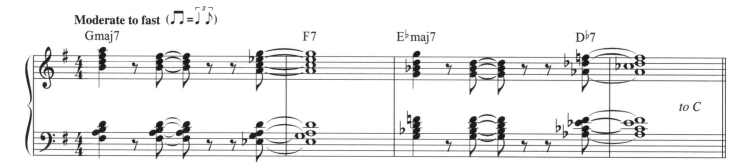

Starting on a II Chord

Intros for tunes that start on IV chords can start on II chords.

| | IIm7 | | V7 | | Imaj7–VIm7 | | Vm7–I7 | ‖ | *to IV* |

Leading to IVm7

Some tunes start on a minor IV chord. A progression leads more naturally to a minor IV chord by using a Vm7♭5 (II of IVm) instead of a Vm7. This example further implies the movement to a minor IV chord by borrowing chords from the minor scale:

| | Imaj7 | | ♭VIImaj7 | | ♭VImaj7 | | Vm7♭5– I7 | ‖ | *to IV* |

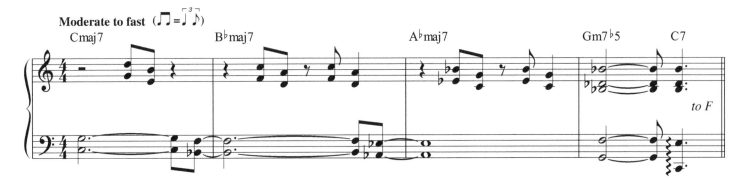

Swing
Minor Keys

Intros in minor keys proceed fundamentally in the same manner as those in major. Since there is no one minor scale, however, more options are available in minor keys. Most of the intros used for major keys can be adapted to minor. This section will offer some sample intros in minor keys. The reader can derive other minor intros from the major intros.

Basic Turnaround Intros

A simple intro can be played on a basic I-V progression:

| Im | V7 | Im | V7 || *to Im*

The V chord can turn into a II-V progression as follows:

| Im | IIm7♭5–V7 | Im | IIm7♭5–V7 || *to Im*

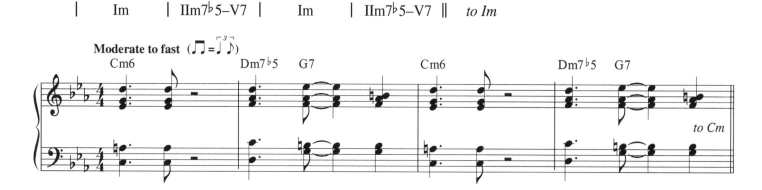

As with major keys, the basic model I-VI-II-V can be used:

|Im6–VIm7♭5 | IIm7♭5–V7 | Im6–VIm7♭5 | ♭VI7–V7 || *to Im*

28

Descending Bass Lines

Descending bass lines are common in minor keys.

The following example progresses from I through ♭VI to V with a descending bass line:

| Im–Im7/♭VII | ♭VI7–V7 | Im–Im7/♭VII | ♭VI7–V7   ‖ *to Im*

The next intro features a descending bass-line elaboration of the Im chord:

| Im–Im /VII | Im/♭VII–Im/VI | VImaj7 | V7   ‖ *to Im*

In the following example, the descending bass line is harmonized with different chords. Notice the parallel movement of the first four chords:

| Im–VIIm7 |♭VIIm7–VIm7| ♭VImaj7 | V7   ‖ *to Im*

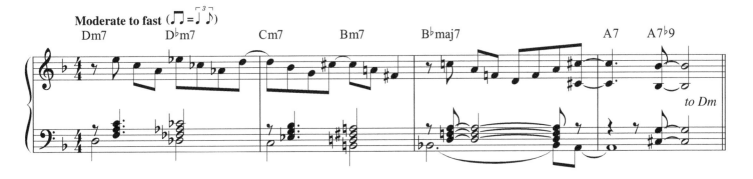

The following example is an eight-measure intro that features a descending bass line. The progression here is fairly elaborate.

| Im–Im7/VII | VIm7♭5–II7 | Vm–Vm7/VI | IIIm7–VI7 |
| IIm7♭5–IIm7♭5 /I | VIIdim7–V7 | Im7–IIm7 | IIImaj7–V7 ‖ *to Im*

The next two examples feature descending bass lines that use a II-V of VI (♭VIIm7-♭III7) movement:

| Im6–VIIm7 | ♭VIIm7–III7 | VImaj7 | IIm7♭5–V7 ‖ *to Im*

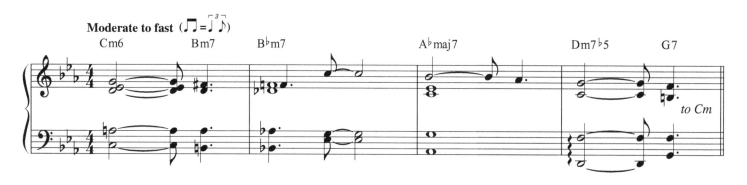

| Im7–VIIm7 | ♭VIIm7–III7 | VI7 | V7 ‖ *to Im*

Chromatic Inner Voice Movement

Minor progressions often feature a chromatic line moving up from, and back to, the fifth of the I chord. Two examples follow:

| Im | | Im♯5 | | Im6 | IIm7♭5–V7 ‖ *to Im*

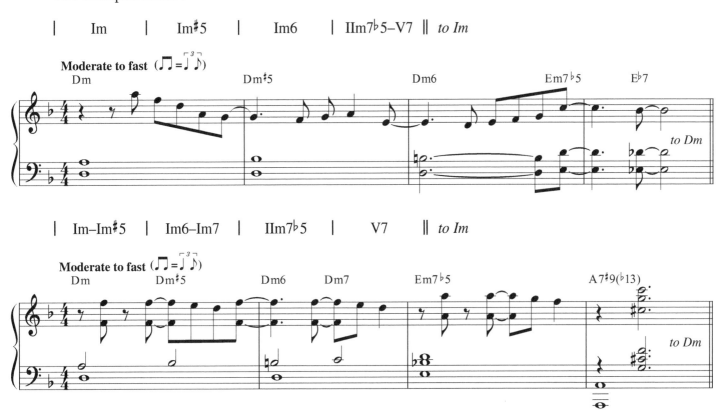

| Im–Im♯5 | Im6–Im7 | IIm7♭5 | V7 ‖ *to Im*

Variations on Major Key Progressions

Variations on standard major-key progressions can be used for intros in minor keys.

This progression hovers around the relative major (A♭ major) before deciding on the tonic minor (F minor). The second and third measures use a II-V-III-VI progression in A♭ major. It is analyzed in F minor:

| Im | IVm7–V7 | Vm7–Im7 | II7–V7 ‖ *to Im*

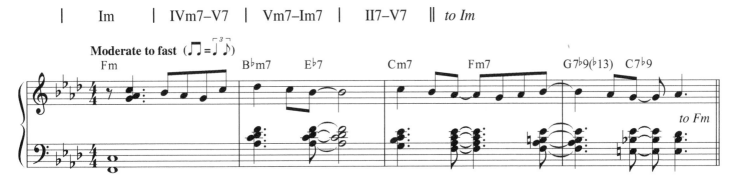

The next example presents a minor variation on a common major progression:

| Im6 | IVm7 | ♭IIIm7–♭VI7 | IIm7♭5–V7 ‖ *to Im*

Circle of Fifths Progressions

The following two examples are based on circle of descending fifths progressions:

| Im6 | IVm7–VII7 | IIImaj7–♭VImaj7 | IIm7♭5–V7 ‖ *to Im*

| Im–IVm7 | VII7–IIImaj7 | ♭VImaj7–♭VI7 | IIm7♭5–V7 ‖ *to Im*

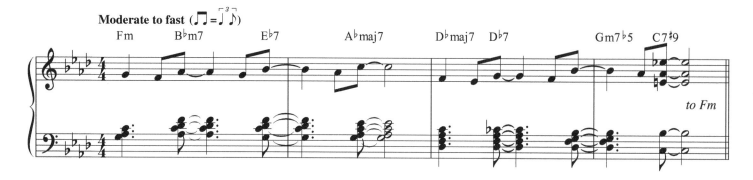

Starting On and Approaching II

Intros in minor tonality for tunes that start on I chords can begin on a II chord, as they do in major. Approaching a II chord at the start of a tune, however, is more problematic in minor than it is in major. Since the II chord in minor is a m7♭5 chord, the approach from a VI7 chord does not establish a temporary V-I relationship as the V7- IIm7 progression does in major. The IIm7♭5 chord cannot be heard as a stable harmony aproached by a dominant 7th chord. Therefore, the IIm7♭5 chord at the start of a tune is best set up by ending the intro on a I chord, or a chord a half step above or below the II chord. All of the following three examples begin on IIm7♭5 chords to help secure the II chord as the start of a tune.

The next two intros are identical except for the last measure. The V7 chord at the end of the first example implies movement to a I chord. A tune starting on a II chord, however, could also be approached in this manner. The absence of the V7 chord in the second example implies more of a movement to II since the intro ends on a I chord.

| IIm7♭5–V7 | Im6–♭III7 | ♭VI7 –V7 | Im–V7 ‖ *to IIm7♭5 or Im*

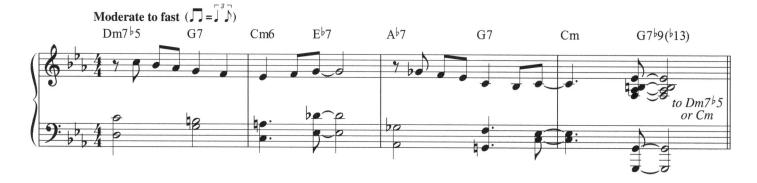

The following intro approaches II through a ♭IImaj7 chord:

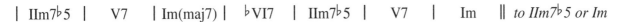

| IIm7♭5 | | V7 | Im(maj7) | ♭IImaj7 ‖ *to IIm7♭5*

Next is an eight-measure intro that features a two-measure break. The intro can lead to a tune starting on a II or a I chord:

| IIm7♭5 | | V7 | Im(maj7) | ♭VI7 | IIm7♭5 | | V7 | | Im ‖ *to IIm7♭5 or Im*

Swing
Vamps and Pedal Tones

Many intros consist of pedal tones and/or vamps. *Pedal tones* are notes that are held under changing harmonies. The most common kind of pedal tone is played on the fifth degree of a scale. This is known as a dominant pedal tone. In this case the fifth degree of the key is held or repeated in the bass while chords change on top. These chords may or may not be derived from the dominant, and almost anything is possible. *Vamps* are repeating patterns that are open-ended; that is, they may repeat indefinitely. Of course, many intros can be repeated, but vamps are designed to do so.

Major Keys

Four variations on a common pedal-tone vamp follow. These examples are based on a dominant suspended 4th sound. The chords are essentially suspended 4th voicings and passing chords over a dominant pedal. These examples are best suited as intros for tunes that start on II chords.

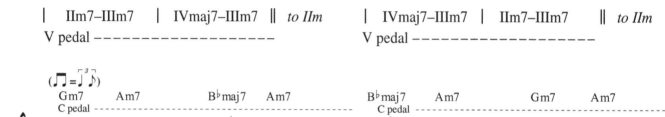

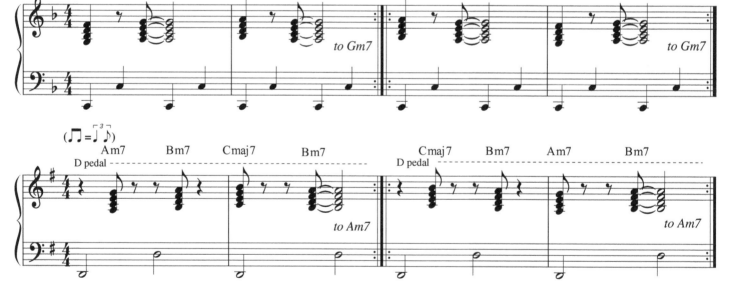

The examples above can be adjusted on the final repeat to better lead to a I chord. In the following examples, the last chord from the first two vamps above is changed to a dominant 7th. A similar adjustment can been made to the other two examples above.

The following two examples on a dominant pedal lead to a I chord.

| Imaj7 | IIm7 || *to I*

V pedal — — — — — — — — — — — — — — —

| IIm7 | V7 || *to I*

V pedal — — — — — — — — — — — — — —

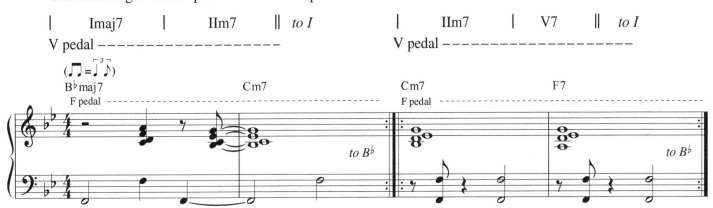

The following intro is based solely on a V7sus or a IIm7 over a dominant pedal tone and leads naturally to a I chord.

| IIm7/V | | | || *to Im*

The following intro is suited for a tune in major that starts on a IIm7♭5 chord, since it features a repetitive IIm7♭5-Imaj7 progression.

| IIm7♭5 | Imaj7 | IIm7♭5 | Imaj7 || *to IIm7♭5*

V pedal — — — — — — — — — — — — — — — — —

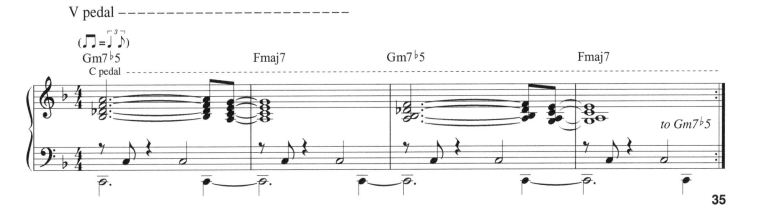

The following two examples feature alternating I and V sus chords as open-ended vamps. These vamps can serve as a background for right-hand improvisations. The following intros offer sample improvisations.

This first example leads to a I chord:

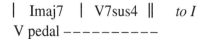

| Imaj7 | V7sus4 ‖ *to I*

V pedal – – – – – – – –

The next example leads to a II chord:

| IIm7 | IIIm7 | IIm7 | IIIm7 ‖ *to IIm7*

V pedal – – – – – – – – – – – – – – – – – –

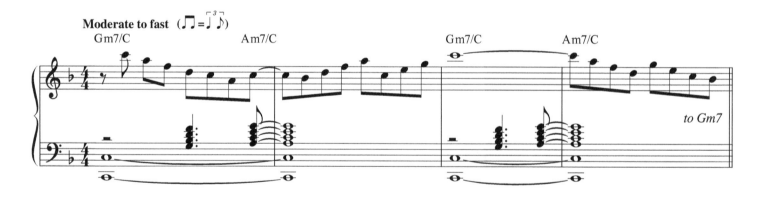

Standard turnaround formulas over dominant pedal tones can be used for intros as well as turnarounds. Two examples follow:

| IIIm7–♭III7 | IIm7–♭II7 ‖ *to I* | IIm7–♭IIIdim7 | IIm7–V7 ‖ *to I*

V pedal – – – – – – – – – – – –   V pedal – – – – – – – – – – – –

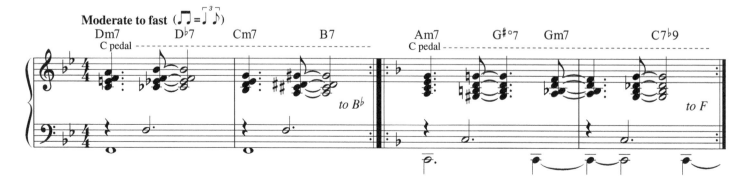

Standard turnarounds without pedal tones are often used for intro vamps. Two samples follow:

| III7–VI7 | II7–V7 ‖ *to I* | Imaj7–VI7 | II7–V7 ‖ *to I*

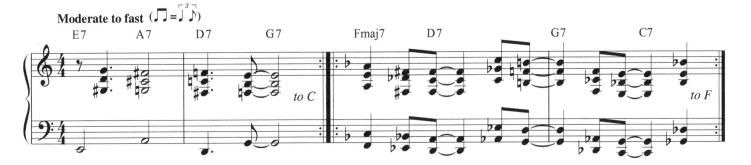

Alternating Parallel Chords

Many vamps consist of alternating parallel chords that are a half step or whole step apart. Dominant 7th chords can be used as I chords in intros even if they lead to a Imaj7 or I6. The following two intros can lead to I chords:

| I7 | ♭VII7 ‖ *to I* | I7–VII7 | ♭VII7–VII7 ‖ *to I*

The following two intro vamps can lead to a I chord or a II chord:.

| I7 | ♭II7 ‖ *to I or IIm* | Imaj7 | ♭IImaj7 ‖ *to I or IIm*

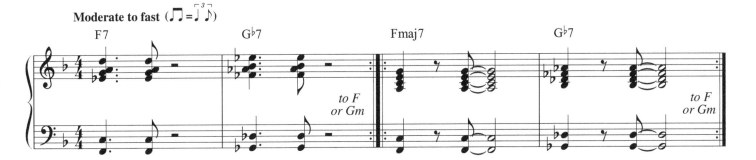

Minor Keys

Vamps and pedal tones can be used for minor keys. Two pedal tone vamps follow. The first is really a repeated I chord that acts like a tonic pedal, and the second is a dominant pedal. Both can lead to a I or a II chord.

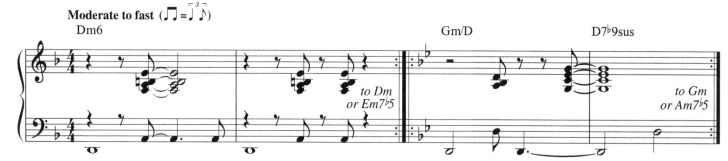

The following two vamps feature half-step movement. The first leads to a I chord. The second can lead to a I or a II chord.

| ♭VImaj7 | V7 || *to Im* | Im6 | ♭II7 || *to Im or IIm7♭5*

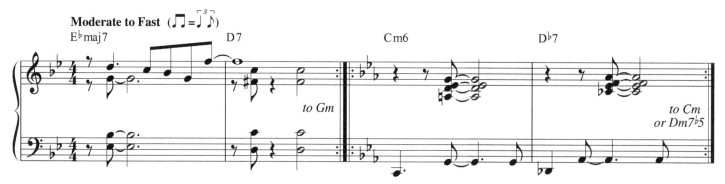

The following four-measure vamp repeats a II-V progression over a dominant in minor and can lead to a I chord or II chord.

| IIm7♭5 | V7♭9 | IIm7♭5 | V7♭9 || *to Im or IIm7♭5*
V pedal– –

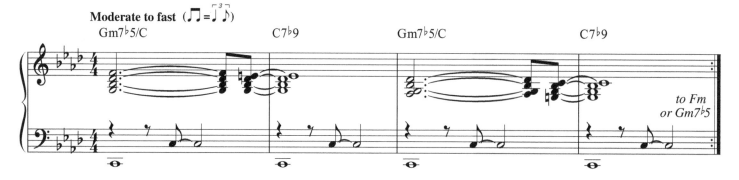

Descending Bass Lines

Many minor vamps consist of descending bass lines. Two variations on a similar progression follow. Both lead to a I chord.

| Im–VI7 | ♭VI7–V7 || *to Im* | Im–Vm/♭VII | ♭VImaj7–V7 || *to Im*

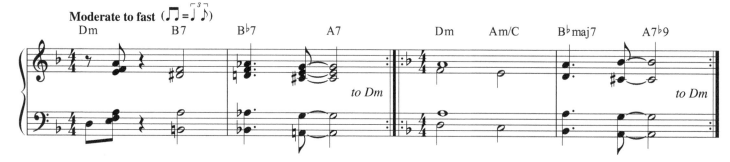

The following two vamps can lead to a I chord or a II chord:

| Im–III7/♭VII | ♭VImaj7–♭II7 ‖ *to Im or IIm7♭5* | Im–Im /VII | Im/♭VII–Im/VI‖ *to Im or IIm7♭5*

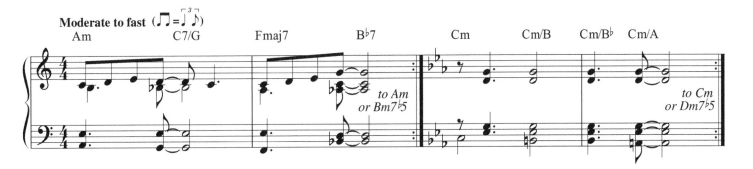

Stepwise Inner-Voice Movement

Many minor vamps contain half-step inner-voice movement.

The following two examples contain the half-step movement 5-♯5-6-♯5:

| Im | Im♯5 | Im6 | Im♯5   ‖ *to Im*

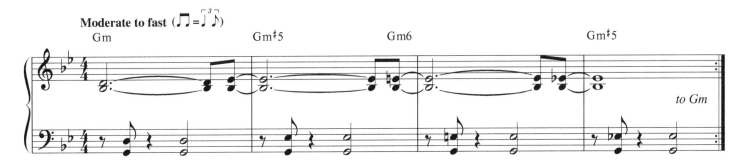

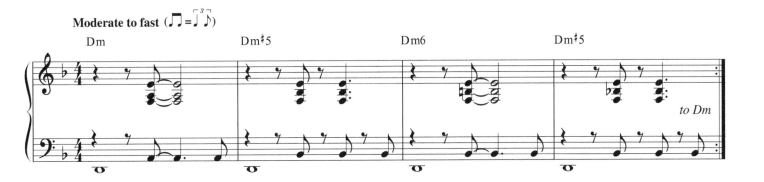

Ballads

Several intros for ballads or slow tempo tunes have been given in the previous sections. This section offers some intros for very slow ballads that can be played rubato or freely ad lib. For a slow ad-lib introduction, almost anything is possible, as long as it sets up a serious mood and implies at least the first chord of the tune. Any of the progressions used in the previous sections can work, as well as many others. A few samples follow.

The following example leads to a I chord. It features static repetition on a single note.

| Imaj7–♭IIImaj7 | ♭VImaj7–♭IImaj7 ‖   to I

The next example features a stepwise descending chord progression leading to a I chord:

| Imaj7–♭VIImaj7 | ♭VImaj7–V7 ‖   to Im

The next example features arpeggiated motion in the right hand part and is based on a standard progression leading to a I chord.

| Imaj7–VI7 | IIm7–V7 ‖   to Im

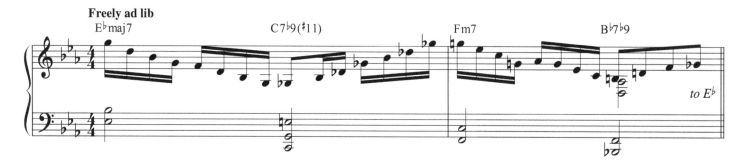

The next example features arpeggiated motion in the left-hand part and leads to a I chord.

| IIIm7 | VI7 | IIm7 | V7 ‖ *to I*

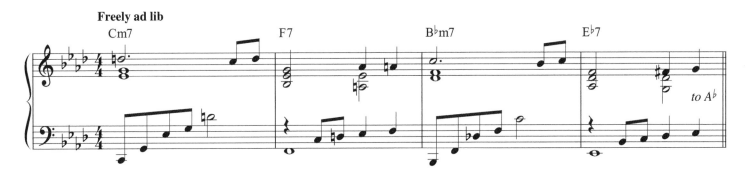

The next example is in minor. It features arpeggios in the left-hand part and leads to a I chord.

| IIImaj7–♭IImaj7 | ♭VImaj7–V7 ‖ *to IIm7*

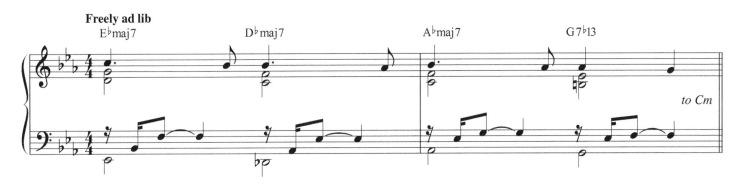

The next example leads to a IIm7 chord.

| Imaj7–♭VImaj7 | ♭IImaj7–VI7 ‖ *to IIm7*

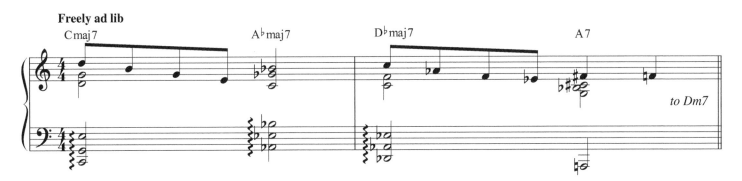

The next intro uses parallel 13th chords and leads to a I chord.

| II7–I7 | ♭VII7–♭VI7–V7 ‖ *to I*

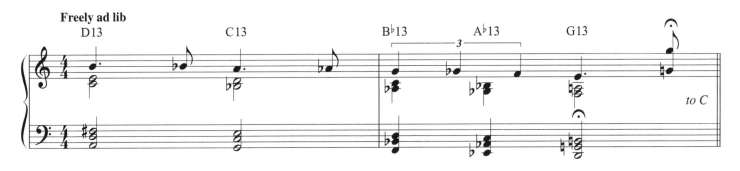

The next example is a variation on a famous eight-measure intro.

| ♭Vm7♭5 | VII7 | IIIm7♭5 | VI7 | IIm7♭5 | V7 | Im | ♭VI7–V7 || *to Im*

Latin Tunes

Traditionally, Latin tunes use intros that differ harmonically as well as rhythmically from standard swing tunes and ballads. Setting up a rhythmic feel is the focus of these intros. Often the intros used are harmonically static and either stay on one chord or alternate between two chords. These intros can be played for four measures as written, or as open-ended vamps. Any of the intros given thus far can be adapted to a Latin style, and the reader should try to invent some. The intros in this section will focus more on those suited to Latin feels. The Latin feels used here are from more of a generic jazz-based idiom than traditional authentic Latin styles like mambo, rumba, etc. All of these examples are suited to bossa nova and related feels.

MAJOR KEYS
Intros For Tunes That Start on I Chords

Alternating I and V7sus chords are often used for Latin vamps. An example follows:

| Imaj7 | IVmaj7/V | Imaj7 | IVmaj7/V ‖ *to I*

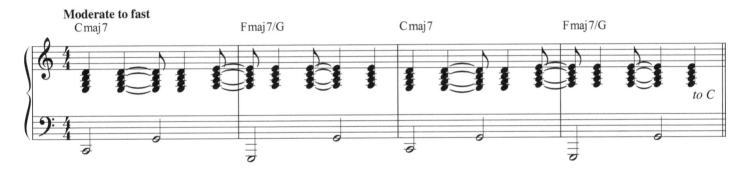

Progressions alternating I and ♭VII chords are common. Two examples follow:

| Imaj7 | ♭VIImaj7 | Imaj7 | ♭VIImaj7 ‖ *to I*

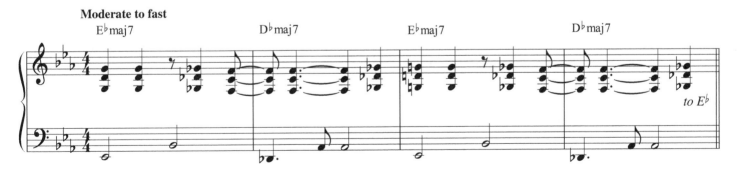

43

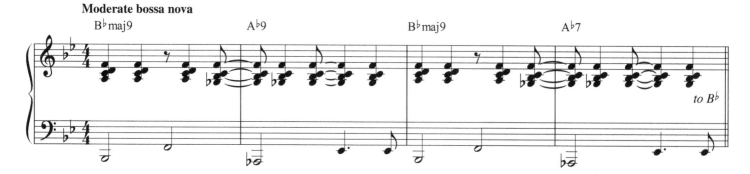

Intros with I-♭II progressions are common. An example follows:

| Imaj7 | ♭II7♭5 | Imaj7 | ♭II7♭5 ‖ *to I*

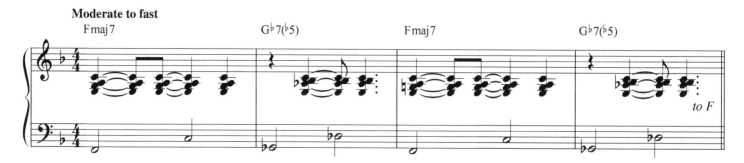

Beginning on a II Chord

The following intro begins on a II chord and leads to a I chord:

| IIm7–Imaj7 | ♭VII7 | IVmaj7–IIIm7 | Im7–V7 ‖ *to I*

Beginning on a I Minor Chord—II-V Vamps

Even though a tune may be in a major key and start on a major I chord, a minor I chord is often used in the intro. A typical Latin vamp alternates Im7 and IV7 chords (II-V of ♭VII). This progression is common in salsa and montunos.

| Im7–IV7 | Im7–IV7 | Im7–IV7 | Im7–IV7 ‖ *to I*

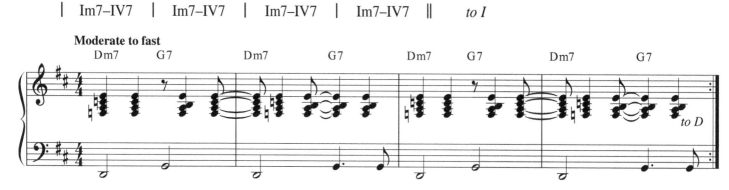

Latin intros can begin on II or V7 suspended 4th chords. The montuno-type intro used above in D major can serve equally as well as a II-V progression in C major.

This next example is essentially the same as the previous, except that here it is a repeating II-V progression in C major instead of a Im7-VI7 progression in D major. Also, the last chord has been changed to D♭7 (tritone substitution).

| IIm7–V7 | IIm7–V7 | IIm7–V7 |IIm7–V7–♭II7 ‖ *to Imaj7*

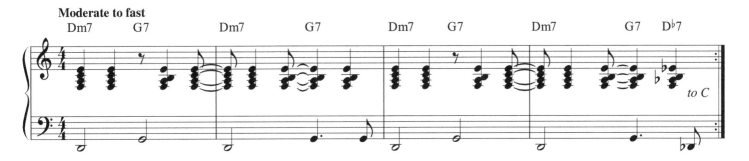

The following example relies on a dominant pedal tone:

| IIm7–V7 | IIm7–V7 | IIm7–V7 | IIm7–V7 ‖ *to Imaj7*
V pedal –

Minor Vamps

Two-measure vamps are common in minor keys. Four examples follow:

| Im6–♭II7 | Im6–♭VII7 ‖ *to Im* | Im–Vm7♭5 | IIm7♭5–V7 ‖ *to Im*

| Im | IIm7♭5–V7 ‖ *to Im* | Im | ♭VI7–V7 ‖ *to Im*

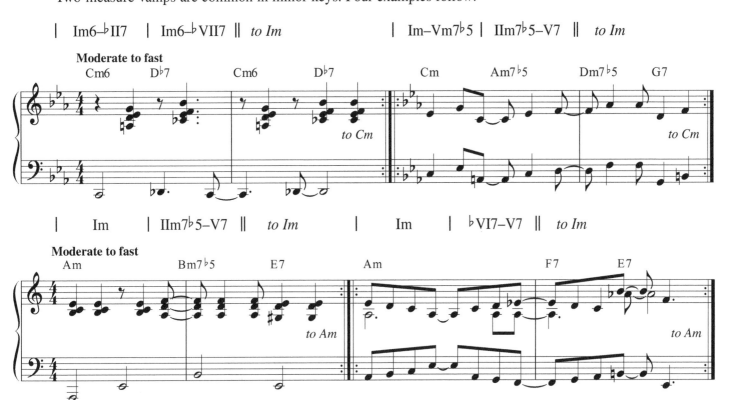

45

Tunes Starting on Other Chords

The following typical Latin pattern can serve as an intro for a tune that starts on a II chord:

| IIm7–V7 | IIm7–V7 | Imaj7–I6 | Imaj7–I6 ‖ *to IIm*

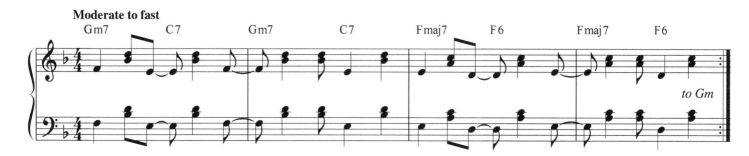

The following intro can lead to a I chord or back to a III chord:

| IIIm7–VI7 | IIm7–V7 | IIIm7–VI7 | IIm7–V7 ‖ *to I or IIIm7*

The following intro leads to a IV chord:

| Imaj7 | IIm7 | #IIdim7 | I7/III ‖ *to IV*

Other Progressions

The undulating rhythmic nature of Latin music lends itself to more exotic progressions. The following four intros use different progressions and lead to I chords:

| Imaj7 | ♭VI7 | ♭IImaj7 | V7 ‖ *to I*

| ♭VII7 | | V7 | || *to I*

Moderate to fast

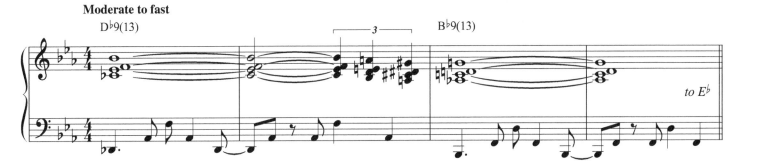

| Imaj7 | ♭V7♭5 | IVmaj7 | ♭VII7–VII7 || *to I*

Moderate to fast

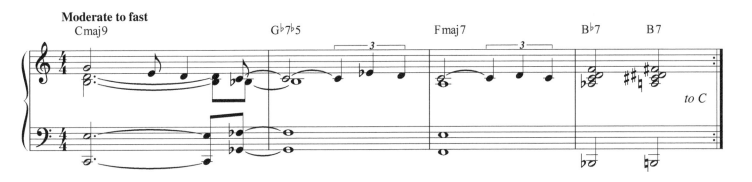

| Imaj7 | IVm7–♭VII7 | IIIm7–VI7 | IIm7–V7 || *to I*

Moderate to fast

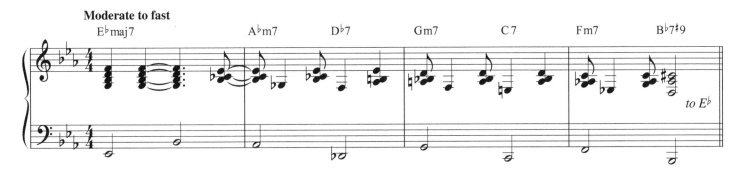

Jazz Waltzes

Jazz waltzes, or tunes in triple meter, make use of almost all of the intro progressions used for swing, ballad, and Latin tunes. As with Latin tunes, the reader should adapt some of these to triple meter. This section will focus on a few intros that are more specific to jazz waltzes.

Vamps

As in Latin music, jazz waltzes are often preceded by a static introduction that alternates two chords. The main purpose is to establish the meter and feel. These intros can be played for four to eight measures or as open-ended vamps. The following four examples alternate two chords and are written as two-measure vamps that could lead to a I or a II chord.

| Imaj7 | V7sus ‖   *to I or IIm* | Imaj7 | ♭II7 ‖   *to I or IIm*

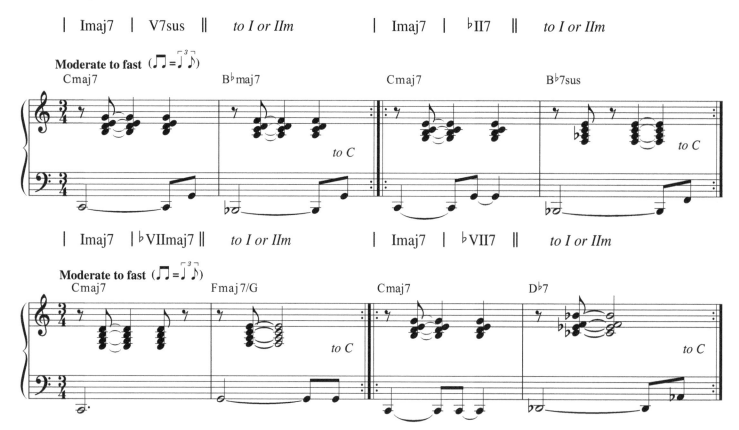

| Imaj7 | ♭VIImaj7 ‖   *to I or IIm* | Imaj7 | ♭VII7 ‖   *to I or IIm*

Pedal Tones

Pedal tones are common in triple meter intros. Two examples follow:

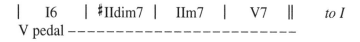

| I6 | ♯IIdim7 | IIm7 | V7 ‖   *to I*
V pedal –

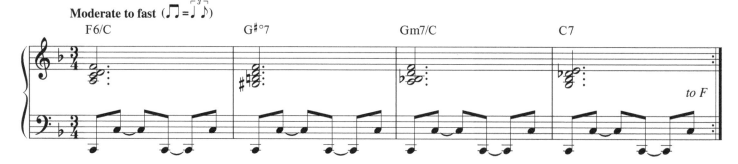

| IIm7 | V7 | IIm7 | ♭II7 ‖ *to I*

V pedal –

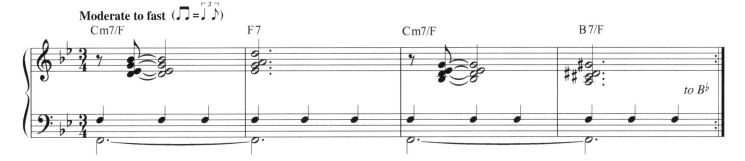

Eight-Measure Intros

Eight-measure intros are common in triple meter, since measures in three are often felt as one macro beat rather than three micro beats.

Typical four-measure turnaround progressions can be repeated to create an eight-measure introduction. The following example descends chromatically from III:

| IIIm7 | ♭III7 | IIm7 | ♭II7 | IIIm7 | ♭III7 | IIm7 | ♭II7 ‖ *to I*

The following intro combines an alternating chord progression with a II-V focus to the tonic.

| Imaj7 | ♭VIImaj7 | Imaj7 | ♭VIImaj7 | IVmaj7 | ♭IIImaj7 | IIm7 | V7 ‖ *to I*

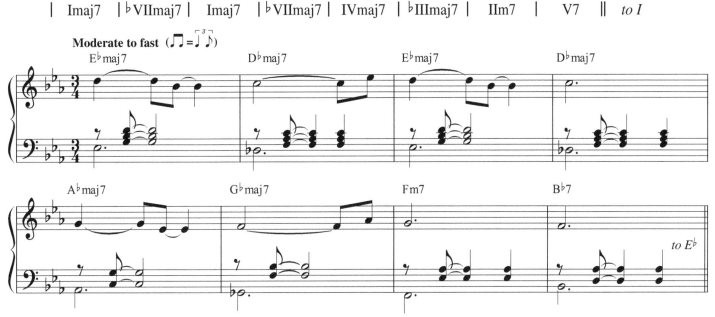

Leading to a II Chord

The following example combines an alternating progression with a III-VI movement that leads to a II chord:

| Imaj7 | IVmaj7 | Imaj7 | IVmaj7 | Imaj7 | IVmaj7 | IIIm7 | VI7 || *to IIm7*

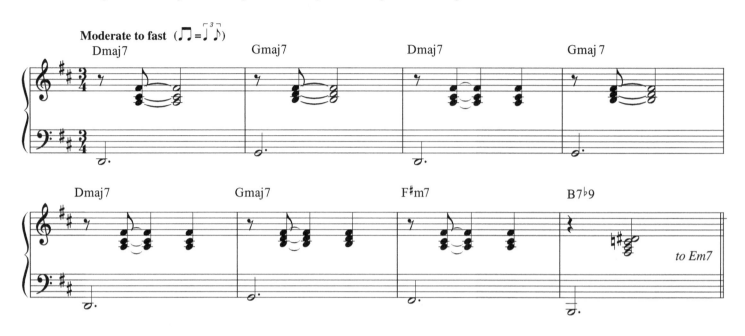

Minor Keys

The following is an eight-measure intro in minor. The progression has more of a sense of movement than the predominately static intros above.

| Im7 | ♭VI7 | V7 | Im6 | Im6 | III7 | ♭VI7 | V7 || *to Im*

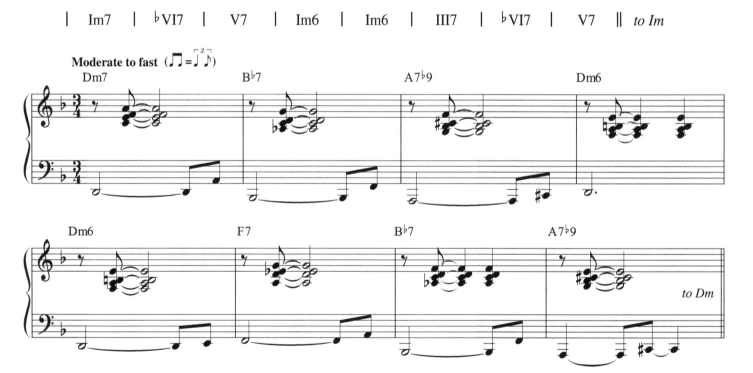

Blues

For more than a century, blues has remained a staple of the jazz/pop repertoire. Although many different genres of blues have evolved (country, urban, jazz, swing, rhythm 'n' blues, rock 'n' roll, etc.), certain traits have remained common in all of them. The following intros are based on "traditional" blues practice and may be applied to several different styles. All of these intros lead to a I chord.

The following two intros are based on a standard blues turnaround progress ion:

| I7–I7/III | IV7–♯IVdim7 | I/V–♭IIIdim7–V7 | I–♭VI7–V7 ‖ to I

| I7–I7/III | IV7–♯IVdim7 | I/V–♭VIm7 | V7–♭VI7–V7 ‖ to I

The next two intros rely on a descending bass line.

| I–I7/♭VII | VIm7–♭VI6 | I/V–♭VI7–V7 | I–V7 ‖ to I

| I7–VII7 | ♭VII7–VI7 | II7–V7 | I–V7 || *to I*

The following example starts on a ♭V7 chord and descends chromatically to a II-V-I progression that leads to I through a ♭II7 chord.

| ♭V7–IV7 | IIIm7–♭III7 | IIm7–V7 | I7–♭II7 || *to I*

The next intro is based on the last four measures of a traditional blues progression. It begins with a V chord.

| V7–♭V7 | IV7 | I | I/V–V7 || *to I*

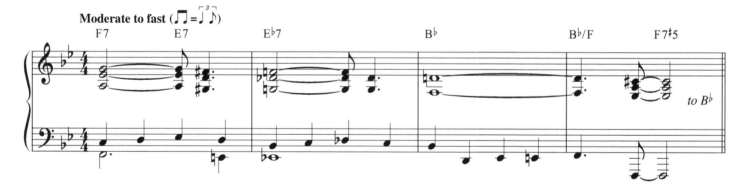

The following intro is based on a typical boogie-woogie pattern. This type of intro was often used by Count Basie.

| I6–#Idim7 | IIm7–V7 | I6–#Idim7 | IIm7–V7 || *to I*

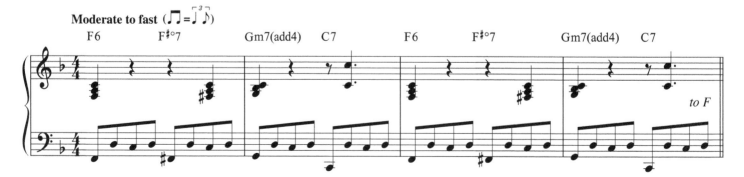

Slower Blues Tempos

The next five examples are intros for slower blues tempos.

The following example begins on a II7 chord and is based on a typical blues ending progression:

| II7–IIIm7–IVm7–♯IVm7 | V7sus4–♭VII7–VII7 | I–VI7 | II7–V7 || *to I*

A variation of the intro above follows:

| IIm7 | V7–♭VIImaj7–VII7 | I–VI7 | II7–V7 || *to I*

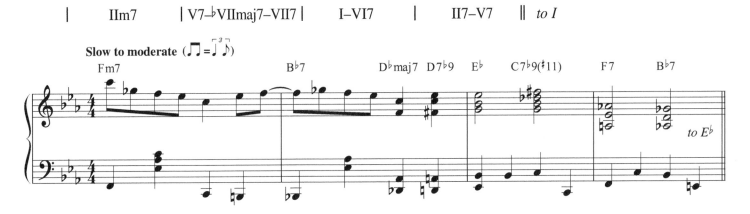

The next intro is in 12/8 and is based on a traditional blues turnaround.

| I6–VI7 | IIm7–V7 | I6–I/III–IV7–♯Idim7 | I6/V–V7 || *to I*

The next intro is also in 12/8 time and is eight measures long.

| I | I7 | IV | #IVdim | I–VI7 | IIm7–V7 | I–VI7 | IIm7–V7 ‖ *to I*

Next is a two-measure intro based on a blues turnaround progression.

| I–I/III–IV–#IVdim | I/V–IIm/VI–VIImaj7 ‖ *to I*

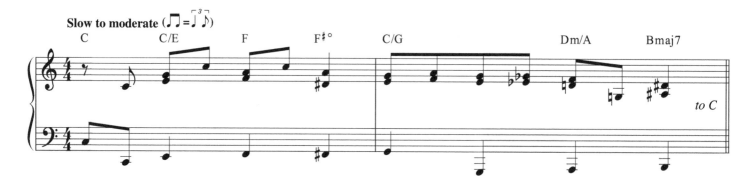

Melodic Considerations and Intros for Singers

A good intro often is derived from the tune itself. Parts of the melody may be used in varying degrees, and motives from the tune can be treated as source material for the introduction. This section will demonstrate a few possibilities from a sample tune. The tune and intros are presented in lead sheet form.

The following is the first eight measures of the sample tune:

The first measure in the following sample intro is from the first measure of the tune, and the last measure is from measure 6.

The next intro is also derived from motives found in measures 1 and 6.

The next intro is derived from m. 5 and m. 6, but uses different chords.

The next example is built around the motive in m. 4 and is less obvious than the others.

When constructing an intro, one should be mindful of whether or not to hint at the upcoming melody. The reader should try to construct motivically derived intros for various well-known tunes.

Intros for Singers

For most singers, one should carefully construct intros so that he or she can find the opening note. How obvious one should make this depends on the skill and experience of the singer.

The following intro, based on the sample tune above, clearly focuses on the starting note E, while leading easily to the opening I chord.

The next intro is more harmonically complex and not related to the tune in an obvious way but the starting note E is consistently on top to cue the singer.

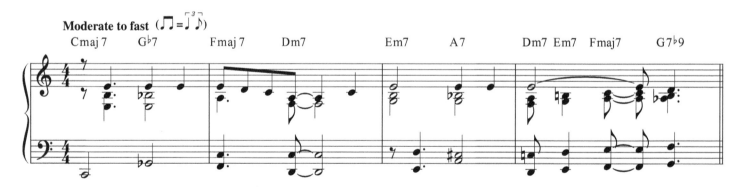

PART 2
ENDINGS

A good ending should bring the music to a satisfactory close. It can be short and abrupt or longer and more gradual. Just as intros set up a mood and tonality at the beginning of a tune, endings should be consistent with both. Over the years a number of standard endings have been used for jazz and pop standard performances.

Set endings are more common than set intros. While intro material may be based on the ensuing tune, endings rarely are. In fact, clichéd endings are and have been shamelessly used by many great artists and arrangers. The reason probably has to do with tradition and familiar closure. A traditional ending clearly signals the listener that "this is it" and cues applause from the audience. Unfamiliar endings might make the listener unaware that it is time to get ready to applaud. Since the listener should be taken into account during any performance, it is a good idea to make an ending obvious if not clichéd. Even great classical works usually end with formulaic endings for the very same reasons.

The endings presneted here are based on traditional practice, but a few original twists are offered. Always keep your audience in mind when constructing an ending.

Swing
Major Keys and Ballads

Two-Measure Endings

Two-measure endings are often used to bring the tune to a quick finish. Here the final cadence arrives shortly after the tune has finished. These endings usually feature a syncopated rhythm.

The simplest two-measure endings use the simplest cadence formula: V-I. The V-I ending is added after the final I chord of the tune, thus the complete ending progression is I-V-I. All of the endings in this section will begin with the final I chord of the tune and proceed with the ending chords. Notice that the quality of the chords can vary.

The following two endings are based on the V-I formula:

| I–V7 | I ||

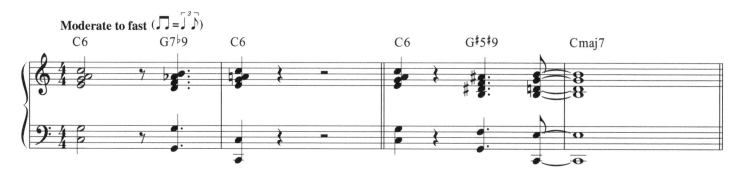

Two-measure endings are often constructed around the tonic chord and a chord whose root is a half step above or below. The following figure contains four examples of endings with tonic and ♭II chords. The ♭II chord can be considered a dominant tritone substitute. Notice that the quality of these chords can vary.

| I–♭II | I ||

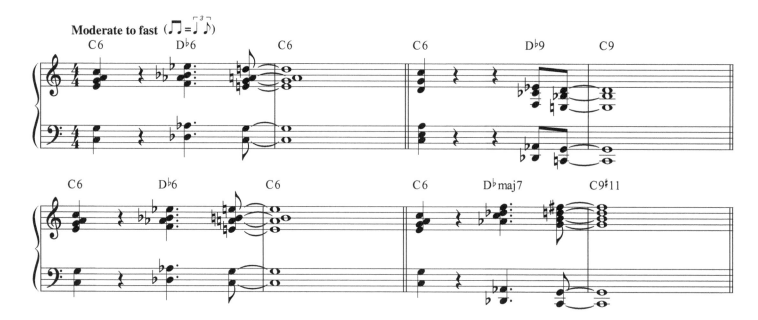

The next figure contains endings that use the tonic and chords that are a half step below, VII chords.

| I–VII | I ||

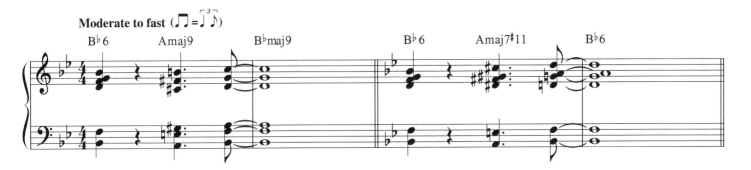

Some endings use three chords by approaching the final tonic through ♭VII and VII chords. Four examples follow:

| I–♭VII–VII | I ||

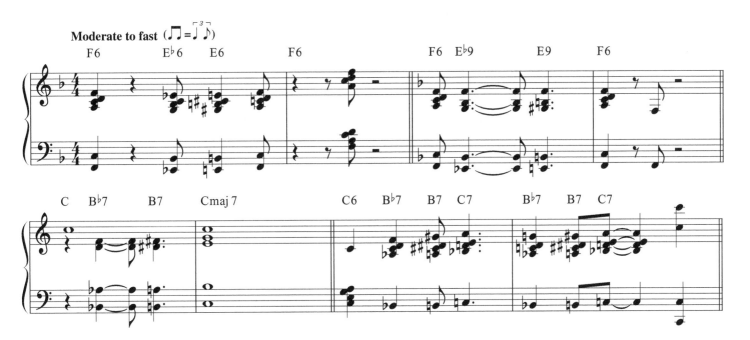

The next two endings approach the final tonic though a ♭VI-V7 progression.

| I–♭VI7–V7 | I6 ||

The tonic of the final cadence may be approached stepwise starting from a chord whose root is a third below or above. Two examples follow:

| I–♭VImaj7–♭VIImaj7 | Imaj7 ‖ | I6–♭IIIdim7–IIdim 7 | I ‖

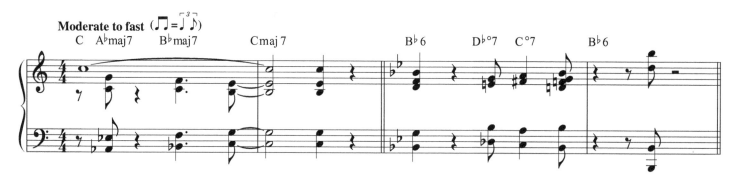

The following two endings feature a decoration of the V chord:

| I6–V7–♭II7 | Imaj7 ‖ | I–♯IVmaj7–V7 | Imaj7 ‖

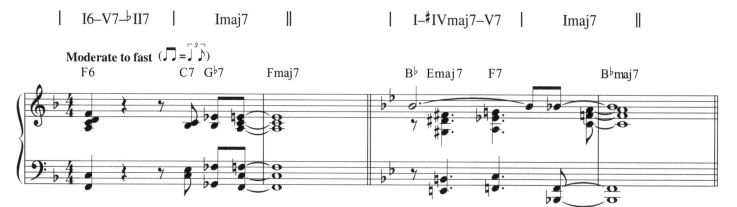

Chromatic progressions are often used for endings. The next figure offers two variations descending from the tonic to the dominant chord.

| I–VII7–♭VII–VI7 | ♭VI7–V7–(♭II7) –Imaj7 ‖

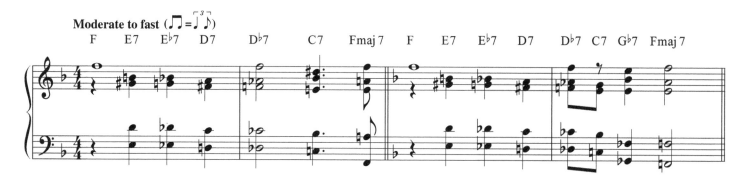

The next two examples feature descending chromatic movement from ♭III and IV respectively.

| I–♭III6–IIm7–♭IImaj7 | I ‖ | I–IV7–III–♭III7 | II–♭II7–Imaj7 ‖

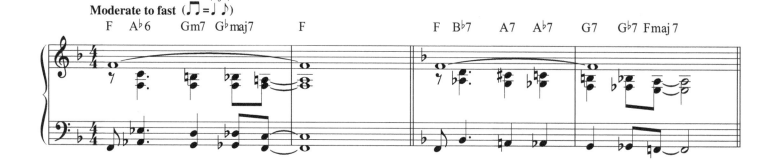

Common Endings

The following is usually referred to as a "Count Basie ending." It is short, to the point, and effective for medium- to up-tempo swing tunes.

Here are to two variants in C major:

| I–IIm7 | ♭IIIdim7–I ‖

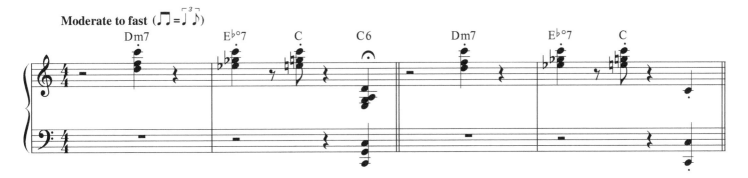

Another common ending for similar situations is the "Duke Ellington ending" made famous in "Take the 'A' Train." Here are two variants in C major:

A descending line is often added above the melody line in the preceding example, and both lines can be played together with harmony as follows:

| I6–I7–IV6–♭VI7 | ♭III7–VIdim7–VIIdim7–Imaj7 ‖

A variation on the descending line of the preceding example can be played in thirds or harmonized with parallel diminished 7th chords.

The following endings are bluesy rhythmic variations on the above examples. The second one is harmonized with parallel dominant chords.

| I7–IV7sus–♭VII7–VI7 | ♭VI7–V7–I7 ‖

Often endings are based on cyclic progressions. Circle of fifths progressions are commonly used. The next figure presents two examples: The first begins the cycle on the tonic chord, and the second begins from a half step below the tonic.

| Imaj7–IV–♭VII7–♭III7 | ♭VI7–♭II7–Imaj7 ‖ | I–VII7–VI7–II7 | II7–V7–I ‖

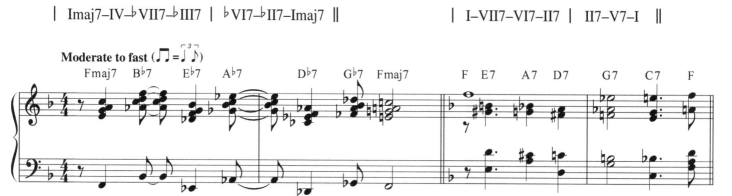

Deceptive Cadences

Many endings begin on chords other than the I chord. The process of resolving to a chord different from the expected tonic is called a *deceptive cadence*. These chords usually harmonize with the tonic note. The final cadence at the end is on the tonic.

The next two endings begin on ♭II and ♭VI respectively.

| ♭IImaj7 | Imaj7 ‖ | ♭VImaj7–♭IImaj7 | Imaj7 ‖

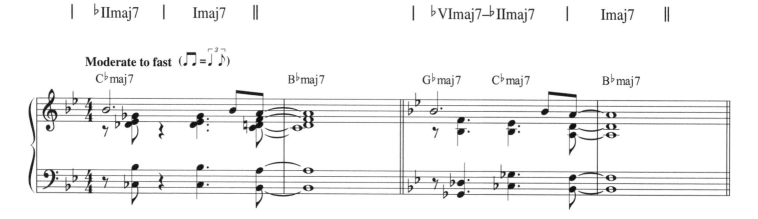

The next two examples begin on IV and ♭V respectively.

| IV7–♭VII7 | I || | ♭V7♭5–IV–III–♭III7 | II7–♭II7–Imaj7 ||

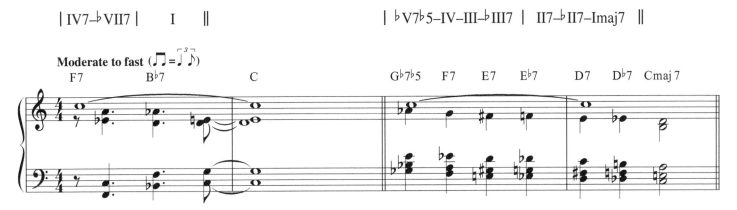

The following ending begins on Vm7 and proceeds chromatically down to I.

| Vm7–♭Vm7–IVm7–IIm7–♭IIIm7 | IIm7–♭IImaj7–Imaj7 ||

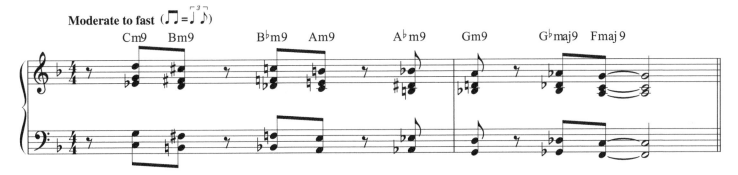

Four-Measure Endings

Four measures or more are often used for endings. The effect in these situations is a more gradual winding down of the tune.

Two common endings based on blues practice follow:

| I–I/♭VII | IV/VI–IVm/♭VI | I/V | V7–I ||

| I–I/III | IV–♭VI/♭V | I/V | V7–I ||

A variation on the first four-measure ending above follows. Notice in the last two measures that the half-step leading tones to notes of the tonic triad are harmonized with diminished 7th chords.

| I–I/♭VII | IV/VI–♭VI7–VIIdim7 | I6–#IVdim7–I/V–♭IIIdim7 | I/III–♭IIdim7–I6 ‖

Two variations on the second four-measure ending follow:

| I6–I/III | IV–#IVdim7 | I/V–IIm7/VI–V7 | I ‖

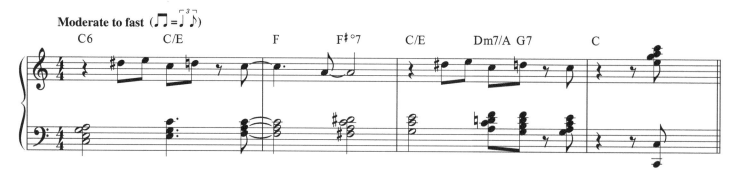

| I6–I/III | IV–#IVdim7 | I/V–♭III7 | II7–V7–I6 ‖

The next two endings are based on circle-of-descending-fifths cycles.

This first one uses all dominant chords:

| I7–IV7 | ♭VII7–♭III7 | ♭VI7–♭II7 | Imaj7 ‖

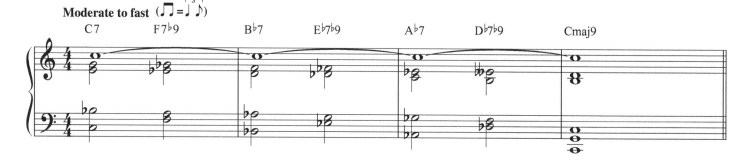

This next example is a variation. It uses II-V movement down the circle of fifths.

| Im7–IV7 | ♭VIIm7–♭III7 | ♭VIm7–♭II7 | Imaj7 ||

A common ending begins on the ♭Vm7♭5 chords and proceeds chromatically down to the tonic. The tonic note is held in the top voice until the last chord, where it can either stay there or move up or down stepwise.

| ♭Vm7♭5–IVm7 | IIIm7–♭III7 | IIm7–♭II7 | I6 ||

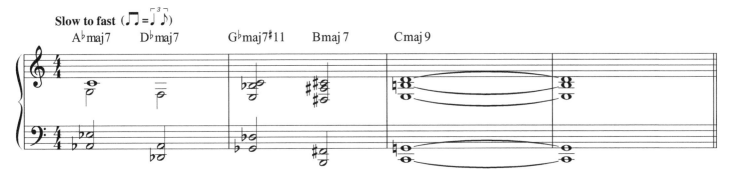

The next two examples are variations on an ending that begins on a ♭VI chord and proceeds down the circle of fifths.

|♭VImaj7–♭IImaj7 | ♭Vmaj7–VIImaj7 | Imaj7 ||

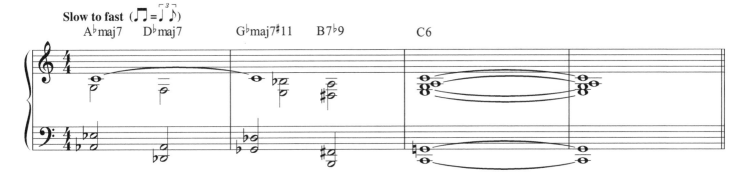

|♭VImaj7–♭IImaj7 | ♭Vmaj7–VII7 | I6 ||

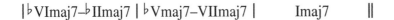

The next example is similar to the two preceding endings but extends the cycle of fifths by beginning on a ♭VII chord.

| ♭VIImaj7–♭III7 | ♭VI7–♭II7 | ♭V7–VII7 | Imaj7 ‖

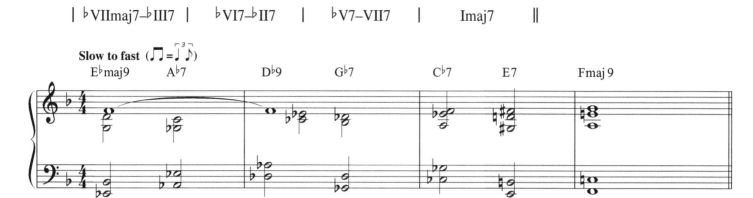

Ballad Endings

All of the ending progressions used thus far can be used for ballads. A few additional sample ballad endings follow.

Deceptive cadence endings are common in ballads. The first one below beings on ♭IImaj7; the second one, on ♭VImaj7.

| ♭IImaj7 | Imaj7 ‖ | ♭VImaj7–♭VIImaj7 | Imaj7 ‖

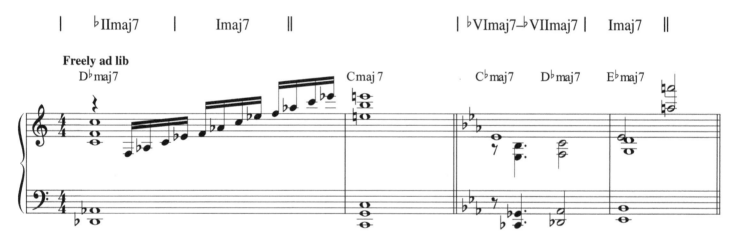

The next ending also uses a deceptive cadence on ♭VImaj7.

|♭VImaj7–♭IImaj7 | Imaj7 ‖

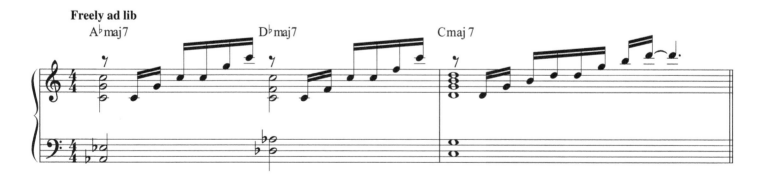

A common four-measure ending follows:

| Imaj7–♭IIIm7–♭VI7 | IIm7–V7 | ♭IImaj7 | Imaj7   ‖

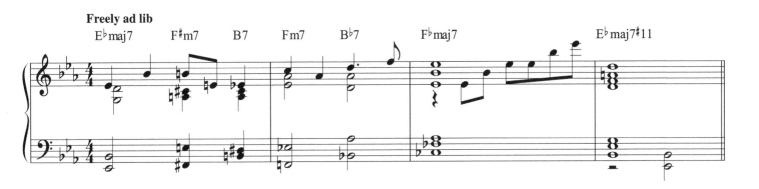

The next ending begins on ♭Vm7♭5 and is a variation on a previously used common up-tempo ending.

|♭Vm7♭5–IV7 | IIIm7–♭III7 | II7–♭IImaj7 | Imaj7   ‖

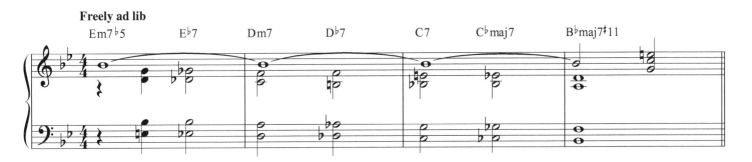

The next ending is in minor and is a common jazz ballad ending.

| Im7–IV7–♭VIIm7–♭III7 | ♭VIm7–♭II7–Im ‖

Swing
Minor Keys

Some of the harmonic formulas used in major-key endings also work in minor keys. The next several minor-key endings are derived from major-key formulas.

Two-Measure Endings

The following two endings are based on a I-V-I progression.

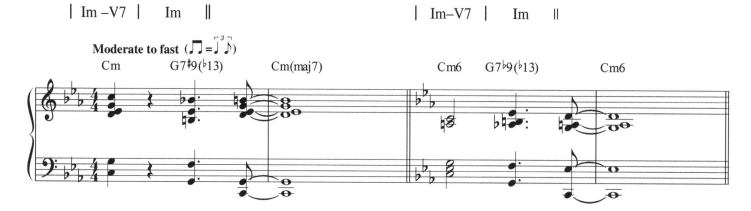

The next two endings are based on a I-♭II-I progression.

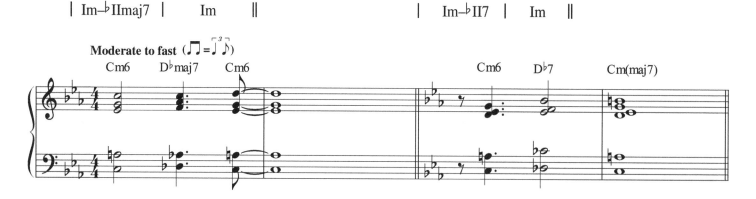

The following two endings use a ♭VI chord before the V chord.

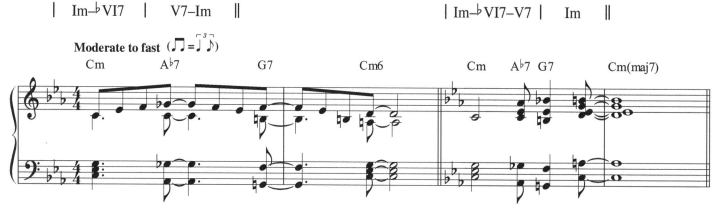

Four-Measure Endings

The following ending is based on minor vamps.

| Im–VI7 | ♭VI7–V7 | Im | ||

The following ending is based on a circle of fifths progression beginning with a ♭VII7 chord.

| Im–♭VII7 | ♭III7–♭VI7 | IIm7♭5–V7 | Im | ||

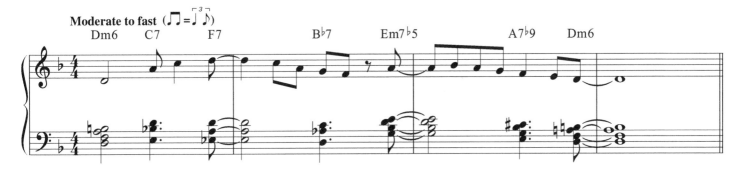

Deceptive Cadences

Deceptive cadences are often used for endings in minor keys. Two two-measure endings follow.

| ♭VImaj7–♭IImaj7 | Im | || | ♭IImaj7–V7 | Im | ||

| ♭Vmaj7♯11 | ♭VI6 | ♭IImaj7 | Im | ||

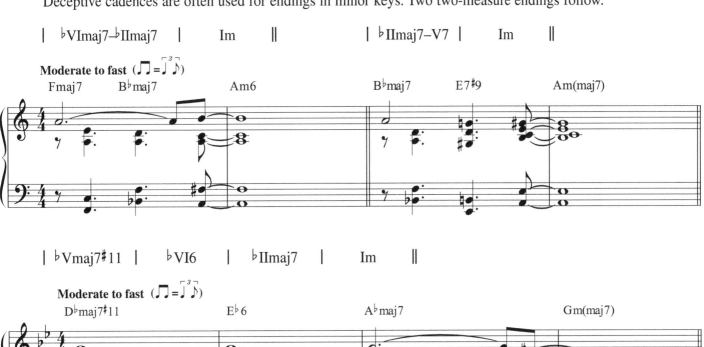

Vamps
Swing, Latin, Jazz Waltz

Vamps are often used for endings in major and minor keys. A vamp may repeat several times before the final ending. Most of the time, the vamps are repeated until a cued ending is attached.

Swing

The following two samples are intro vamps in a swing style that are adjusted for endings. They are in major and minor respectively.

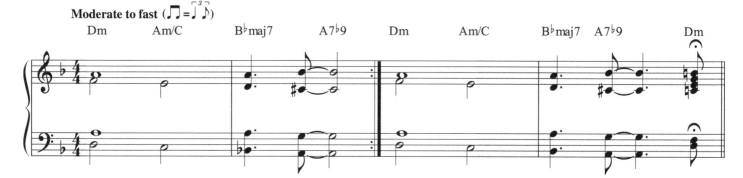

Latin

Many Latin tunes end with vamps that are similar to intros. An example follows.

Jazz Waltz

Jazz waltzes also typically end with intro-like vamps. The next example also features a dominant pedal tone.

| IIm7 | V7 | IIm7 | ♭II7 :‖ Imaj7 ‖

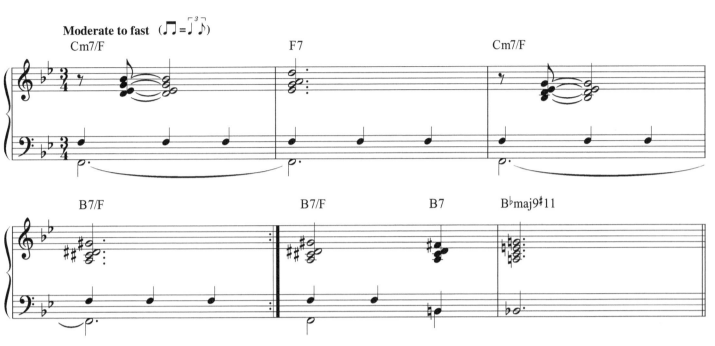

PART 3
TURNAROUNDS

Turnarounds are harmonic progressions that take the music from one chord to another chord. They are usually used in situations when a chord has a duration between two and four measures. Musicians usually insert turnarounds at the end of a tune in order to lead the harmony back to the beginning, or between sections of a tune. Also, turnarounds are often inserted over harmonically static areas within the main body of a tune.

Melodic considerations are important in determining which turnarounds work best in any given situation. Certain common turnarounds have evolved over the years, and this section will present some of them as well as demonstrate the process for creating turnarounds. For easy comparison, all examples are written in the keys of C major or C minor. Only chord symbols are given in these examples. The player must provide his or her own voicings. One should play each example first as chords only, and then with an improvised melody along with the chords. All examples should be transposed to all keys.

I to I Turnarounds

When a tune ends on a I chord and begins on a I chord, rather than sit on a I chord for more than two measures, turnarounds are usually employed. The most basic kind of turnaround leads from a I chord back to a I chord. The following turnarounds lead from I to I during a two-measure span.

Creating Four-Chord Turnarounds

The simplest way of going from I to I is to insert a V chord between them (A). One can easily turn the V chord into a II-V progression (B). The harmonic rhythm can remain consistent with the addition of a VIm7 as a I chord substitute (C). VIm7 is often used as a tonic substitute after the tonic is played since VIm7 shares three notes in common with a Imaj7 chord. With this simple process, one can create a four-chord turnaround in place of one static harmony.

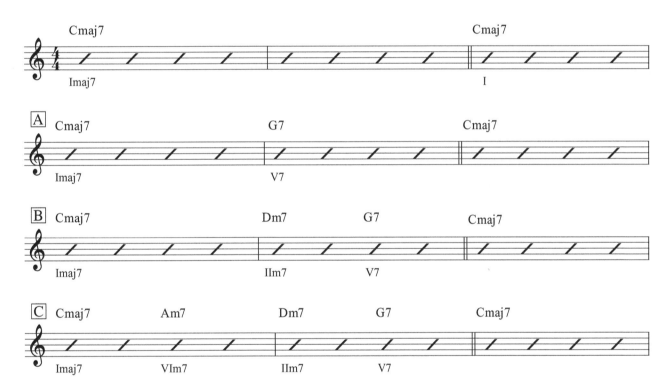

Any chord in this last progression can be approached by a *secondary dominant* chord (a dominant 7th chord whose root is a perfect fifth above), in other words, by its V7 chord. Thus, Dm7 can be approached by A7 (IIm7 by VI7) which in this case would be V of II.

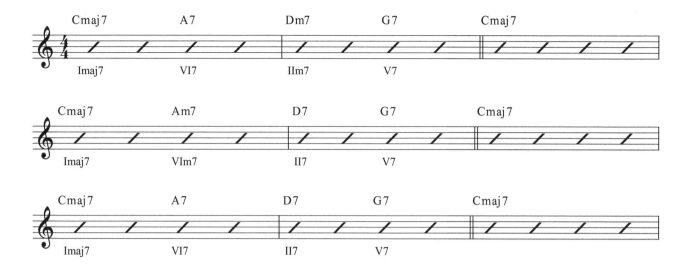

Tritone substitution is an important concept in jazz harmony. The principle most often applies to dominant 7th chords. A tritone substitute is a chord of similar quality whose root is a tritone (augmented fourth or diminished fifth) away from the original chord. Thus a D♭7 can take the place of a G7, or an E♭7 can be used for an A7, etc. In the key of C major, this would be a ♭II7 for a V7 and a ♭III7 for a VI7, etc.

By using tritone substitutions, the last turnaround above could be altered to the following examples:

Tritone substitution can be used with the original Imaj7-VIm7-IIm7-V7 turnaround progression to create more alternatives.

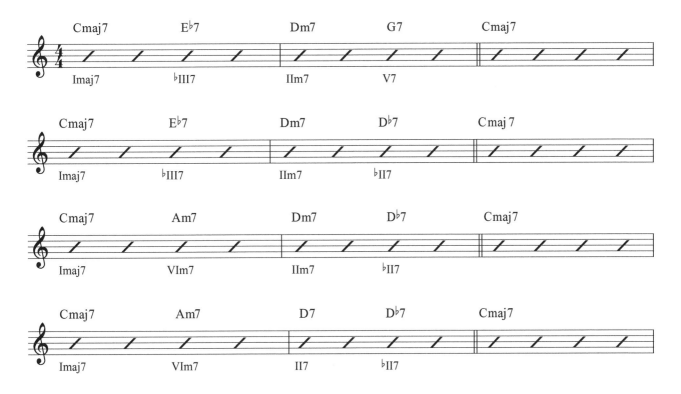

The Imaj7–♭III7–♭VI7–♭II7 from the previous set of examples is often changed to all major 7th chords as follows:

This progression can be mixed with the previous progressions to form various combinations. Several examples follow:

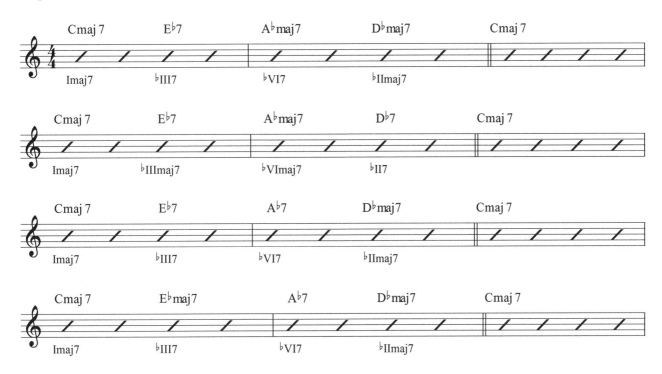

Minor 7th chords can be used on ♭III and ♭VI as tritone substitutes for VIm7 and IIm7 respectively.

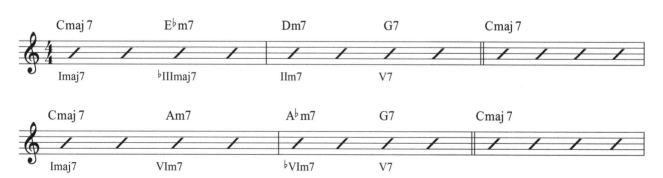

Diminished chords are often used on ♯I and ♭III to lead to the II chord. These chords substitute for VI7 and ♭III7 respectively.

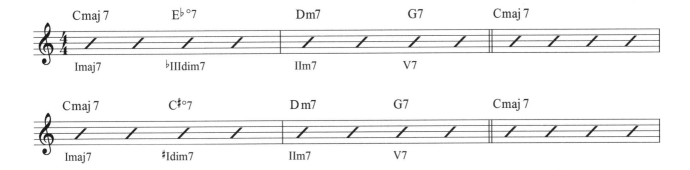

Blues Turnarounds

The following three turnarounds are typically associated with blues styles but may be used in almost any situation.

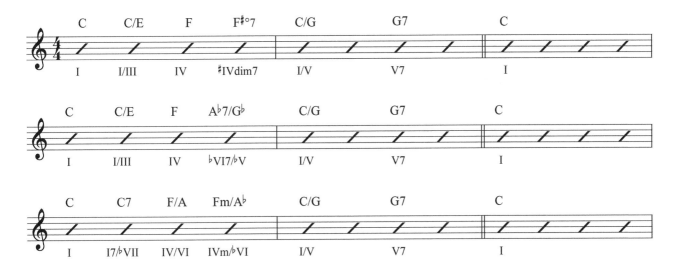

I Chord Substitutes

Many turnarounds that occur between sections of a tune often begin with a IIIm7 chord as a substitute for I. This gives a sense of delayed resolution until the beginning of the next section. All of the previous turnarounds used in this section can be used in this manner by substituting Em7 for the first Cmaj7 chord. Only two samples will follow.

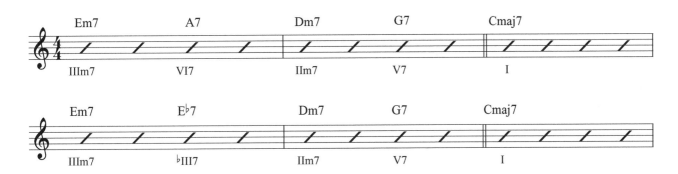

A dominant chord on III (III7) can be used as a substitute for the first I chord in many situations. Two samples follow.

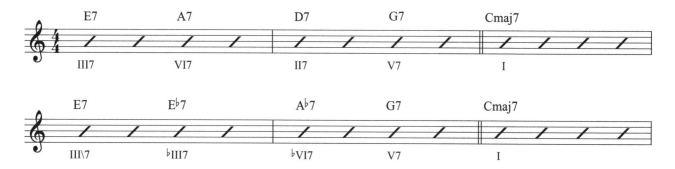

The tritone substitution for III7 can also be used in a similar manner. As with the IIIm7 substitute, this can apply to many of the turnarounds used thus far.

Two samples follow. Notice that through the tritone-substitution principle, the progression is a circle of descending fifths, and the second is a series of descending half steps. With tritone substitution, descending fifths and descending half steps are equivalent.

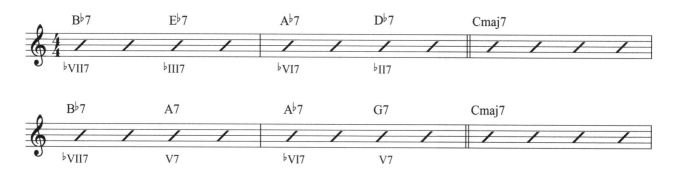

A ♭V7♭5 chord also can substitute for I in some situations.

The ♭V7m7♭5 can be used for a I chord at the beginning of various progressions. Three examples follow.

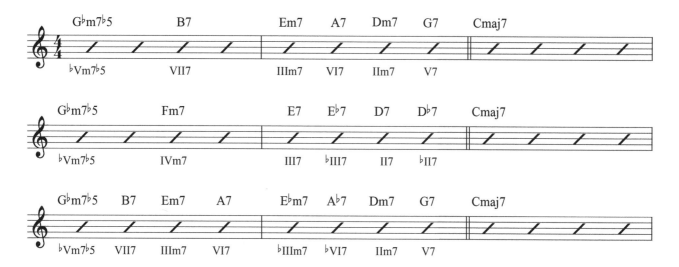

♭VImaj7 can substitute for a I chord at the beginning of a turnaround. Four possibilities follow. Notice the circle of descending fifths and descending half-step progressions.

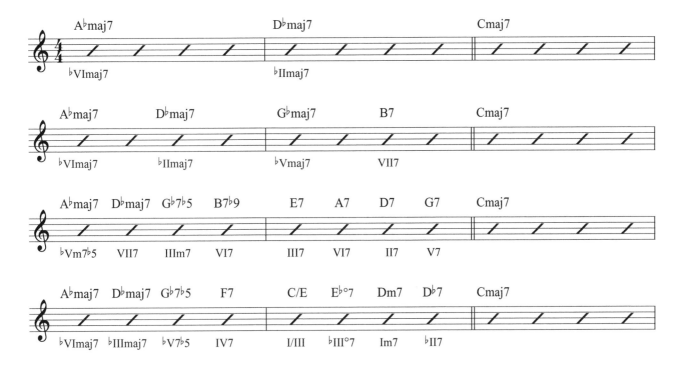

Circle of Fifth Progressions

Each chord in a circle-of-descending-fifths progression leads naturally to the following chord, thus these progressions are ideal for turnarounds. A basic procedure is to think backwards from the target chord. The next three examples present various ways of doing this while holding a common melody note. The assumed held notes in the following three examples are C, G, and E, respectively, in the key of C major.

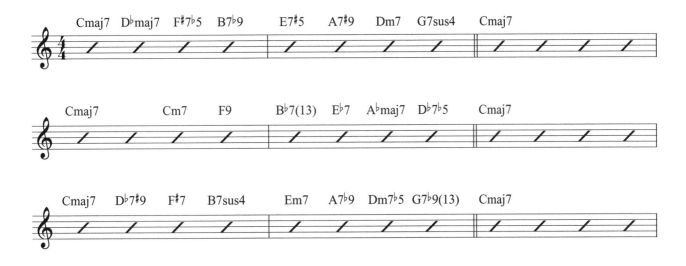

I to II Turnarounds

This section will present turnarounds that lead from a I chord to a II chord. The II chord can be either a minor 7th (IIm7) or dominant 7th (II7) in most cases. Also, a IIm7♭5 is possible in some cases. All three alternatives may be tried for each example.

The simplest way of getting from I to II is through a V7 of II chord (VI7). As before, one can easily turn the V chord into a II-V progression. The following examples demonstrate the process:

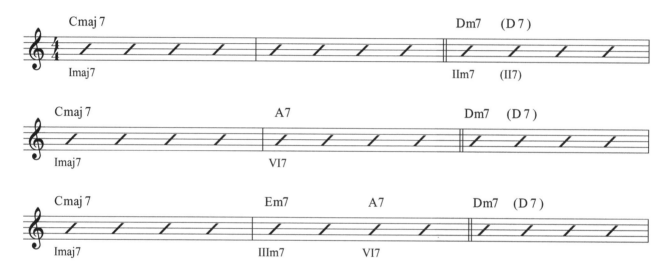

There are various way of going from the I chord to the IIIm7 in the previous example. Three examples follow. The first uses IIm7 as a passing chord. The second uses VII7 as V7 of III. The third uses IV7 as a tritone sub for VII7. This last progression is more commonly used.

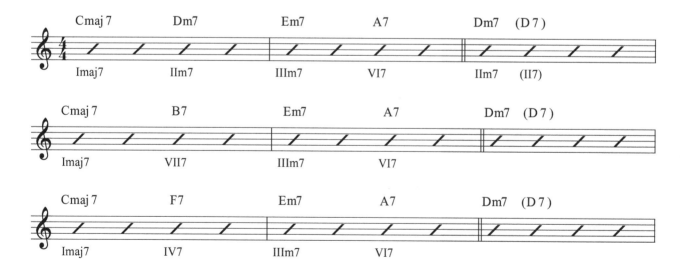

The next series of examples presents variations on the model above. Various substitutions and alternates similar to those used for I to I turnarounds are employed.

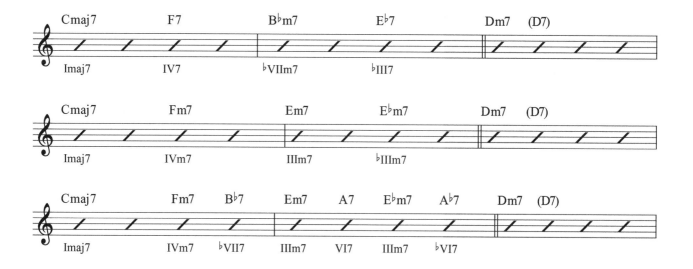

I Chord Substitutes

Substitutes may be used for I to II turnarounds in much the same way that they were for I to I turnarounds. A IIIm7 chord is often used in place of the I chord. The next three examples demonstrate how IIIm7 can be used in place of I. The third example is a common progression that actually leads to V7 through the IIm7 chord.

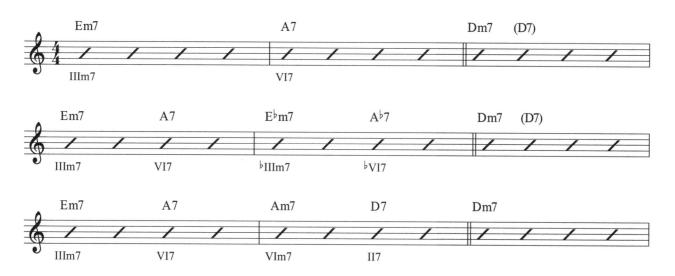

♭Vm7♭5 also is used often in place of a I chord. Three examples follow:

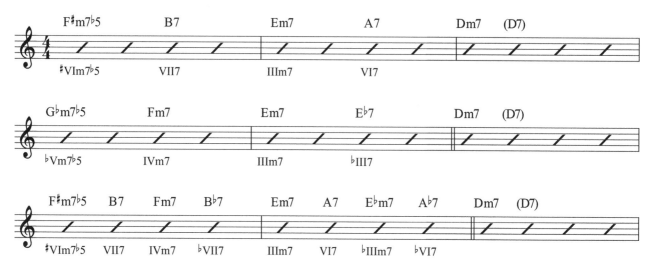

I to IV Turnarounds

This section presents turnarounds that lead from I to IV. The IV chord is usually major but can be also minor. The simplest way of going from I to IV is through V of IV, which happens to be I7. Changing the Imaj7 chord into a dominant 7th chord attains a smooth transition. As before, one can easily turn the V of IV chord into a II-V of IV. The following examples demonstrate the process:

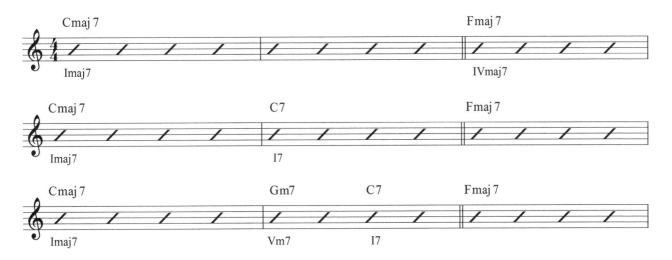

VIm7 can be added after I as a I chord substitute to increase the harmonic motion, as follows:

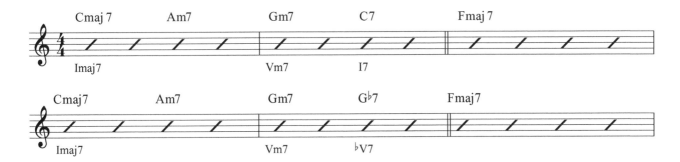

The next series of examples presents variations on the model above. Common substitutions and embellishments are used.

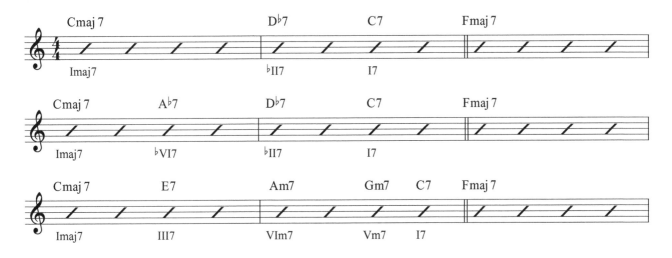

The next example presents an ascending stepwise progression.

The next two examples use tritone substitutions for II-V of IV.

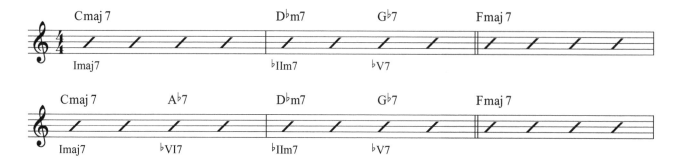

I Chord Substitutes

As before, I is often substituted for by other chords at the beginning of a I to IV turnaround.

The next two examples use VI as the substitute.

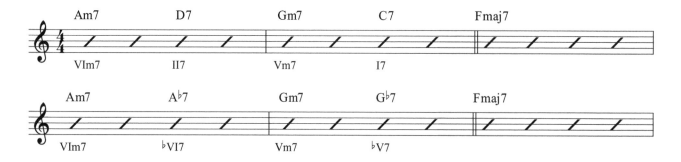

The next two examples use IIIm7 as the substitute.

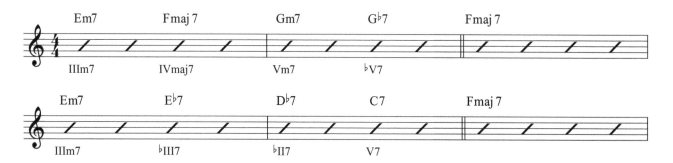

I to VI Turnarounds

Turnarounds that lead from I to VI are presented in this section. The V of VI chord (III7) is the obvious link to the VI chord. As before, the V of VI chord may be changed to a II-V of VI. The following examples demonstrate the process.

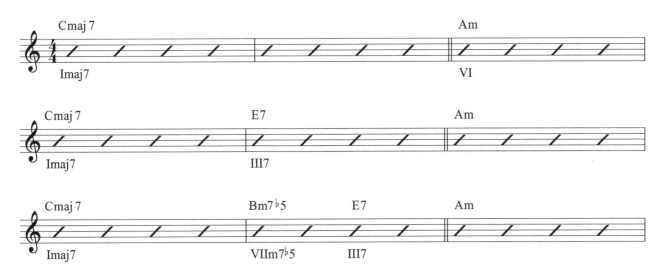

A chord may be added after the I chord to increase the harmonic rhythm. The first example in the next series goes to a I chord substitute (VIm7). The IV chords in the second and third examples complete a circle of descending fifths.

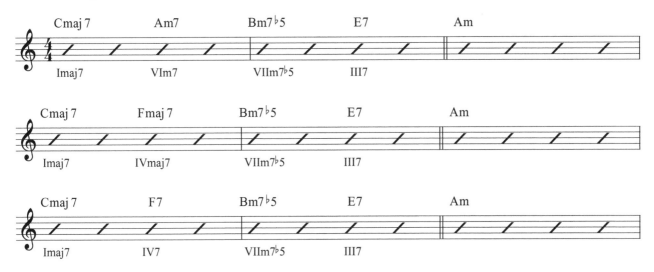

A circle of descending fifths can also be played as follows:

By using tritone substitution one can derive the following turnaround:

The next two examples lead to a IV chord in the second measure before leading to VI through its dominant and dominant tritone substitution.

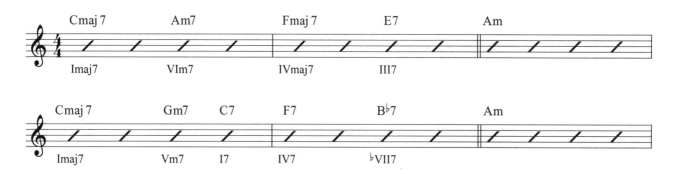

The next example goes through a cycle of II-V chords in descending half steps beginning with ♭IIm7♭5.

I Chord Substitutes

A substitute may be used for the I chord at the beginning of these turnarounds.

The next two examples use a ♭Vm7♭5 chord as the substitute chord.

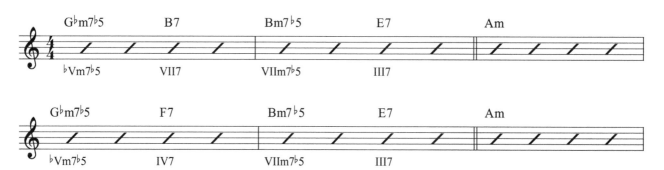

The next two examples use a ♭IImaj7 chord as the substitute chord.

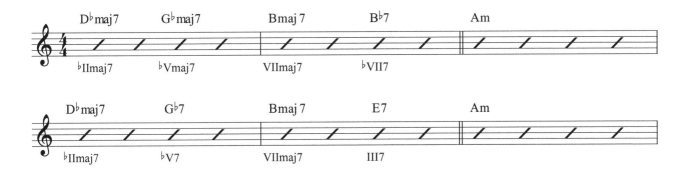

IVmaj7 is used as a substitute for I in the next two examples.

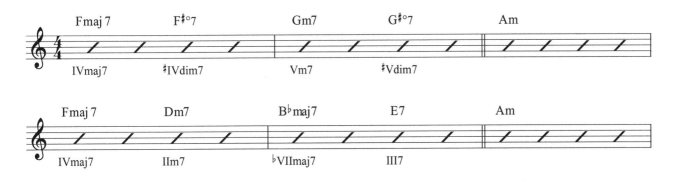

Minor-Key Turnarounds

Turnarounds in minor keys work in a similar manner to those in major keys. However, there are some formulas that do not work. The main differences among chord relationships between major and minor are ♭III and ♭VI chords. While they act as nondiatonic substitutes in major, they are part of the scale in minor. Also, whereas VI and ♭VI occur equally in minor, natural III rarely occurs in minor. By keeping these differences in mind, one can derive minor turnarounds from major turnarounds.

I to I Turnarounds

I to I turnarounds in minor are the most similar to those in major. The ♭III chord is used as a chord on the third degree and as a tritone substitution for VI. A few samples are given here and the reader should infer others from the major key examples.

Turnarounds with descending bass lines are common in minor. Three examples follow:

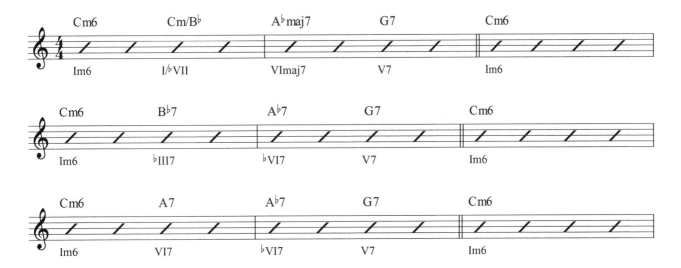

I to II Turnarounds

Turnarounds from I to II in minor are more of a problem. The II chord is a minor 7♭5 and does not tonicize as a minor 7th would. However, several formulas work quite well. A few samples follow.

I to IV Turnarounds

Turnarounds from I to IV in minor work in a similar manner to those in major. Several examples follow.

I to VI Turnarounds

I to VI turnarounds in minor keys are similar to those in major keys. The ♭VI degree is the most often used. Several examples follow:

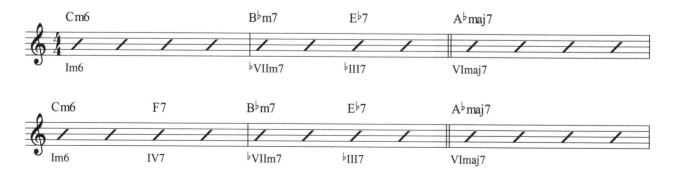

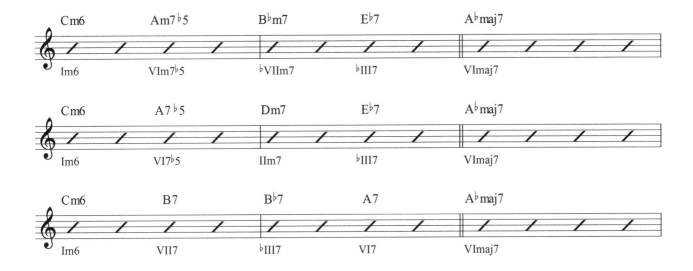

I Chord Substitutes

As with major keys, various chords may substitute for the initial I chord of a turnaround. ♭III and ♭VI are the most common. The reader should try various combinations. Four samples follow:

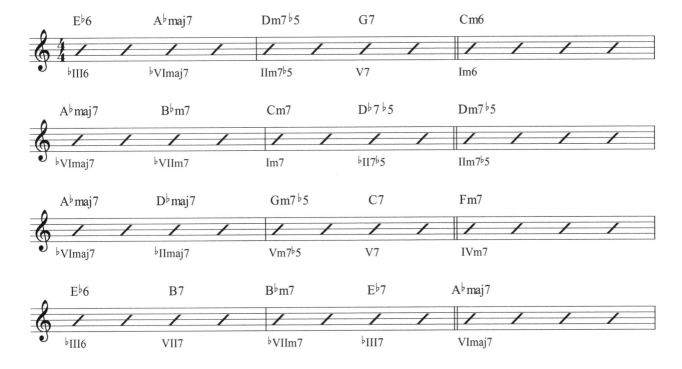

SECTION TWENTY

Tags

Tags are related to turnarounds in that they delay a final resolutaion. Tags are usually played at the end of a tune and suspend the preparation to the final cadence. A tag may consist of (A) a repeating phrase at the end of a tune, (B) a repeating phrase with a tonal shift at the end of a tune, or (C) a deceptive cadence that leads back to the ending phrase. The last alternative is perhaps the most common, and can be repeated indefinitely. The melody may be improvised during this turnaround ending, and often can provide an exciting and dramatic finish to any given performance. after a tag is finished, any ending can be taked on. A sample tune ending and examples of the three tags follow:

Conclusion

One cannot overemphasize the importance of good intros, endings, and turnarounds. They are important for both musicians and listeners. The intro should not only set up the mood and tonality, but also should create a sense of anticipation and act as an invitation to the listener. On a practical musical level, the intro can get a band settled in on tempo, feel, dynamics, etc. before the tune actually begins. While many jazz performances do not use introductions, an intro on the first tune of the night is highly recommended so that things can "feel right" before continuing. Vamp intros are a good means to accomplish this.

Endings are equally as important as intros. While not all tunes will necessarily have intros, all tunes will have endings (apart from fade endings on recordings). Performers should not lose sight of the effect on an audience a good ending can have. Tags can increase the drama of a big finish by delaying the final cadence. Dynamics are an important part of effective endings.

Turnarounds are the heart and soul of jazz harmonic practice. One could analyze almost all jazz chord progressions as a series of turnarounds. The concept of going from here to there in several different ways is at the core of the creative process used in jazz. The blues is a great example of this. There are countless variations on the basic 12-bar blues harmonic pattern. For instance, how one gets from the I chord on the first beat of the first measure to the IV chord on the first beat of the fourth measure can be quite adventurous, and there are many possibilities. One can easily extend the turnaround concept when connecting any two chords. Art Tatum was a master at this, and was very influential in this regard.

The reader should try the various intros, endings, and turnarounds found in this book with various jazz and pop standard tunes to see how they work in different situations. One should categorize each tune by style and first chord used. For instance, the following tunes are in a swing style, are in major and begin on a I chord: "My Romance"; "Bye Bye, Blackbird;" and "It Could Happen to You." The following tunes are in a swing style, are in major, and begin on a VI chord: "All the Things You Are," "Fly Me To the Moon," etc.

This book can be most useful when the reader takes the basic principles presented here and applies them toward new and creative endeavors. Also, one can gain a better aural understanding of heard intros, endings, and turnarounds by relating them to those found in the book.